CUT AND CREATE!

HOLIDAYS

EASY STEP-BY-STEP PROJECTS THAT TEACH SCISSOR SKILLS

Written and illustrated by Kim Rankin

Teaching & Learning Company

1204 Buchanan St., P.O. Box 10
Carthage, IL 62321-0010

This book belongs to

_____

Cover by Kim Rankin

Copyright © 1997, Teaching & Learning Company

ISBN No. 1-57310-083-8

Printing No. 987654321

Teaching & Learning Company
1204 Buchanan St., P.O. Box 10
Carthage, IL 62321-0010

TABLE OF CONTENTS

Shapes 5

Suggestions for Using Some of the Projects 6

Back-to-School . . . . *August* 7

Grandparents' Day . . . . *September* 9

Rosh Hashanah . . . . *September* 11

Yom Kippur Yarmulkes . . . . *October* 14

Columbus Day . . . . *October* 16

Halloween Boo . . . . *October* 18

Halloween Cat . . . . *October* 20

Halloween Pumpkin . . . . . . *October* 23

Election Day . . . . *November* 25

Thanksgiving Pilgrim Hat . . *November* 27

Thanksgiving Turkey . . . . . *November* 29

Hanukkah Menorah . . . . . . *December* 31

Christmas Poinsettia . . . . . *December* 33

Christmas Deer . . . . *December* 35

Christmas Santa . . . . *December* 37

Christmas Tree . . . . *December* 40

Kwanzaa . . . . *December* 42

Martin Luther King, Jr. Day . *January* 44

Groundhog Day . . . . *February* 47

Valentine Bear . . . . *February* 49

Presidents' Day . . . . *February* 52

St. Patrick's Day . . . . *March* 54

April Fools' Clown . . . . *April* 56

Easter Bunny . . . . *April* 59

Easter Basket . . . . *April* 62

Earth Day . . . . *May* 64

Cinco de Mayo Sombrero . . *May* 67

Cinco de Mayo Serape . . . . *May* 69

May Day Flowerpot . . . . . . *May* 71

Mother's Day . . . . *May* 73

Flag Day . . . . *June* 75

Father's Day . . . . *June* 77

Fourth of July . . . . *July* 80

Dear Teacher or Parent,

"I did it myself" is a phrase which can be the foundation for a lifetime of accomplishment and positive self-esteem.

Cut and Create activities can be used by the teacher or parent to develop a variety of important early skills and to provide projects in which children can take pride and succeed.

- Simple patterns and easy, step-by-step directions develop scissor skills and give practice in visual-motor coordination. The scissor rating system in the upper right-hand corner on the first page of each project quickly identifies the easiest projects (✂), moderate (✂ ✂) and challenging (✂ ✂ ✂).
- Materials used are inexpensive and readily available.
- Finished products are fun, colorful and have myriad uses from play items to props; room decorations for walls, bulletin boards or mobiles; learning center manipulatives for counting, sorting, classifying or labeling; gifts or favors for parties or guests; and much more.

The simple and fun activities included in this book will help young learners build a solid base for a variety of skills such as: following directions, observation, discrimination and information processing. A variety of learning styles is addressed including visual, auditory and tactile.

Your art program, whether structured or serendipitous can benefit from these simple and sequenced scissor skill activities. You students will

- develop manual dexterity
- communicate
- learn to control his or her environment by being responsible for tools and materials
- observe
- discriminate (by color, shape, texture)
- sort, order, group and engage in other math processes
- imagine!

We hope you and your students will enjoy these projects. They have been designed to stimulate learning and creativity in a way that is simple and fun. So go cut and create! And have a good time!

Sincerely,

Kim

Kim Rankin

SHAPES

Shapes are seen and used in everyday life. You can find them on street signs, houses, windows and rooftops. Notice the shape of a box of crackers, the crackers and a plate. Look at books, desks, floor tiles and shelves. The patterns in this book utilize many basic shapes and reinforce familiarity with their forms and names.

 **Circle** is round or the shape of a plate.

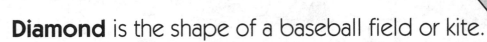 **Diamond** is the shape of a baseball field or kite.

 **Heart** is a popular shape at Valentine's Day.

 **Octagon** is the shape of a stop sign.

 **Oval** is the shape of an egg.

 **Rectangle** is the shape of a door.

Stars may have many points. This star has five points.

 **Square** is the shape of a saltine cracker.

 **Teardrop** is the shape of a raindrop.

 **Triangle** is the shape of a roof on a house.

Welcome to Mrs. Smith's Class

Different Uses

- Mobiles
- Tabletop or Desk Decorations
- Party Favors
- Take-Homes for Parents
- Refrigerator Magnets (Reduce 25-40%)
- Ceiling Decorations
- Window/Door Decorations
- Greeting Cards (Reduce 30-40%)
- Portfolio Pieces
- Folders (Reduce 30-50%)

Bulletin Boards

Use whatever design you need for the particular season or holiday you will be displaying. You may want to enlarge the patterns for your bulletin board or door.

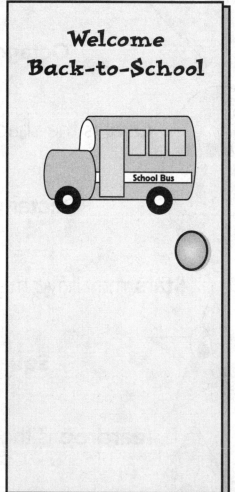

Greeting Cards

Celebrate a holiday or create an occasion. Handmade greeting cards are a surefire hit for parents, grandparents, relatives and friends. And what better way to say "thank you" to a visitor, custodian, principal, helper, etc.

Materials: black, brown, pale yellow, peach, red, tan and white paper; scissors; glue; black crayon or marker

BACK-TO-SCHOOL

AUGUST

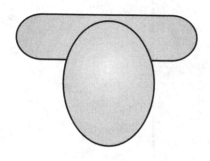

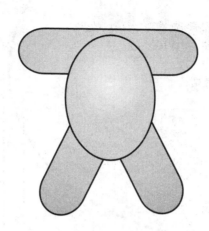

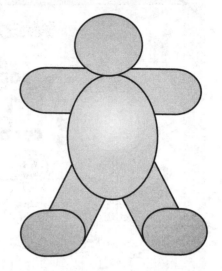

1 Cut one #1 body and #2 arms from whatever color you choose for your person. Glue together as shown.

2 Cut two #3 legs and add to the bottom part of the body.

3 Cut two #4 feet and glue to the legs as shown. Cut one #5 head and glue to the top of the body.

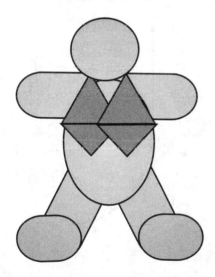

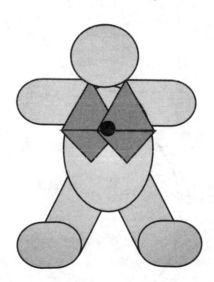

4 Cut two #6 and #7 vests from whatever color you want to make the vest. Glue in place as shown. (Note: You can make up your own outfit for your person.)

5 Cut one #8 button from black paper or draw a button on with a marker.

6 With a marker, make a face or cut one out from colored paper. (Note: Make several different color people and glue them together holding hands. These make great coatrack or cubby tags.)

BODY
1
CUT ONE

ARMS
2
CUT ONE

LEGS
3
CUT TWO

FEET
4
CUT TWO

HEAD
5
CUT ONE

VEST
6
CUT TWO

VEST
7
CUT TWO

BUTTON
8
CUT ONE

Note:
This is how the face is rendered.
Use this to trace or copy.

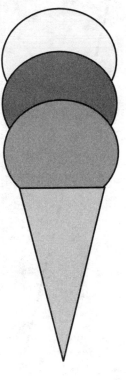

1 Cut one #1 cone from tan paper.

2 Cut three #2 ice cream scoops from three differ- ent ice cream colors. Glue the first color ice cream to the back of the cone. Glue the second behind the first scoop of ice cream and so on.

3 Write *You are the coolest!* on the first scoop. (Note: You could use a brown marker to make a waffle pattern on the cone.)

You are the coolest!

Note: Cut the scoops from colors that represent favorite flavors. Make a graph to show the most popular flavors in your class.

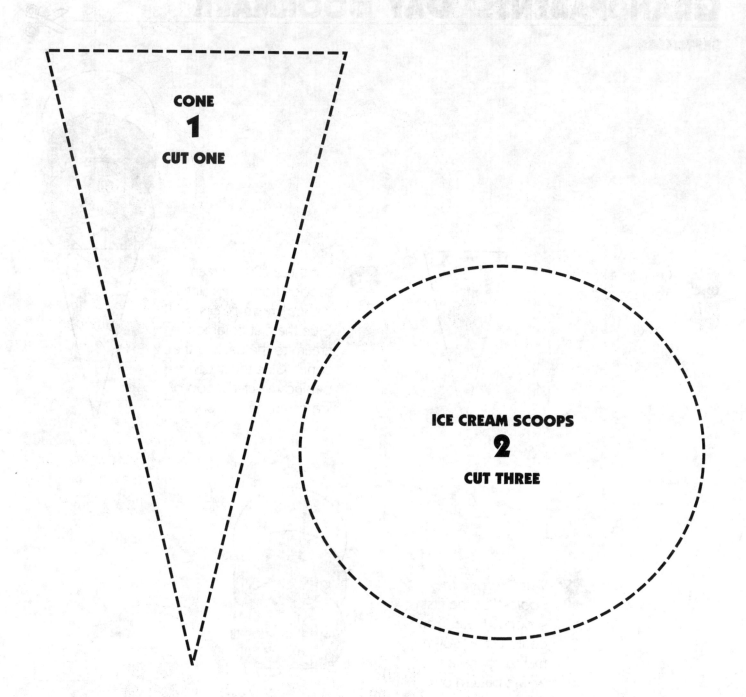

CONE

1

CUT ONE

ICE CREAM SCOOPS

2

CUT THREE

You are the coolest!

Note:
Copy or use these letters to trace onto the ice cream.

Materials: *black, brown, green, golden yellow or tan, ivory or pale yellow and white paper; scissors; glue; black crayon or marker*

ROSH HASHANAH

SEPTEMBER

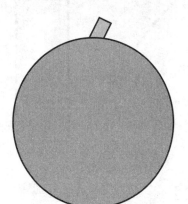

1 Cut one #1 apple from red paper. Cut one #2 stem from brown paper and glue to back of the apple.

2 Cut one #3 middle from white paper and glue in the center of the apple.

3 Cut one #4 leaf from green paper and glue behind the stem. Cut one #5 core from pale yellow or ivory and glue in the middle of the apple. Draw a line down the center of this piece with a marker. Cut six #6 seeds from black paper. Glue three on each side of the center line as shown. (Note: You could use real apple seeds.)

4 Cut one #7 honey pot from tan or golden yellow paper and glue to the side of the apple as shown.

5 Cut one #8 base from tan or golden yellow and glue to the bottom of the honey pot.

6 Cut one #9 lid from tan or golden yellow and glue to the top of the honey pot. With a marker, write *Honey* on the pot.

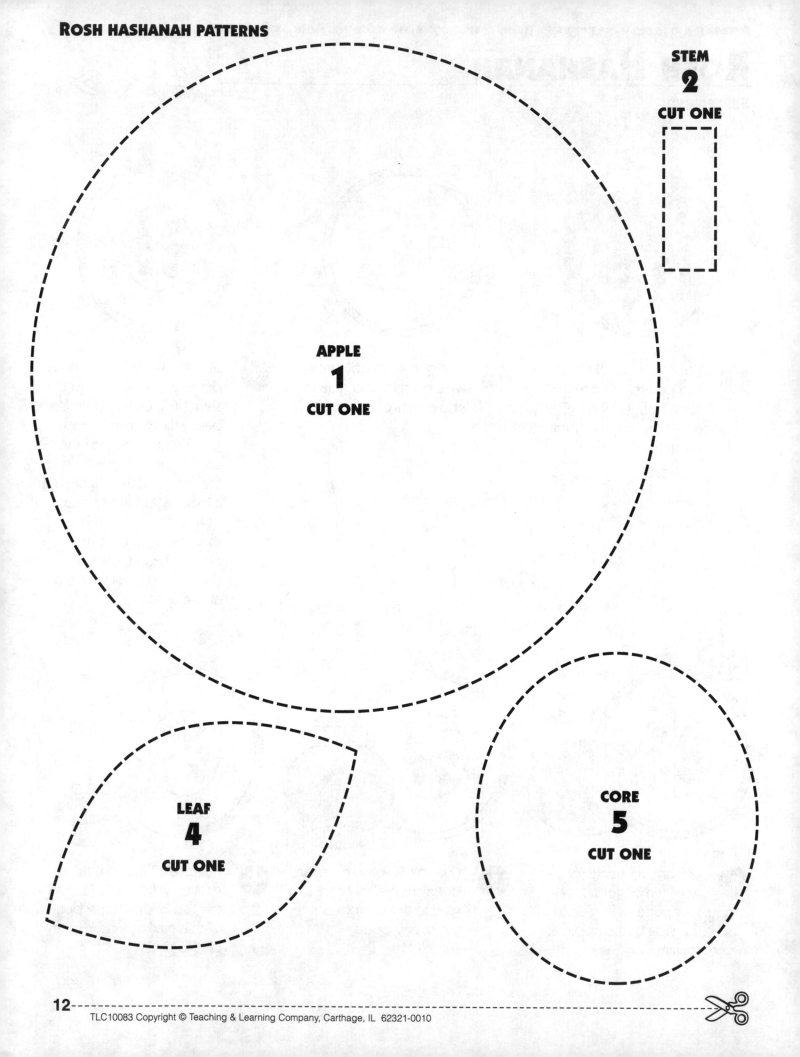

STEM

2

CUT ONE

APPLE

1

CUT ONE

LEAF

4

CUT ONE

CORE

5

CUT ONE

SEEDS
6
CUT SIX

MIDDLE
3
CUT ONE

BASE FOR HONEY POT
8
CUT ONE

LID FOR HONEY POT
9
CUT ONE

HONEY POT
7
CUT ONE

Honey

Note: Copy or use these letters to trace onto the honey pot.

YOM KIPPUR YARMULKES

OCTOBER

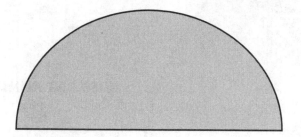

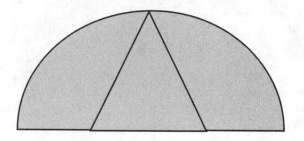

1 Cut one #1 cap from light blue paper. (These caps can be made from any color.)

2 Cut one #2 center from light blue paper. Glue to the cap as shown.

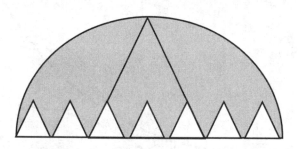

3 Cut seven #3 triangles from white paper. Glue at the bottom of the cap as shown.

Note: These pattern pieces can easily be cut from felt for an attractive, more permanent take-home item or gift.

YOM KIPPUR YARMULKES PATTERNS

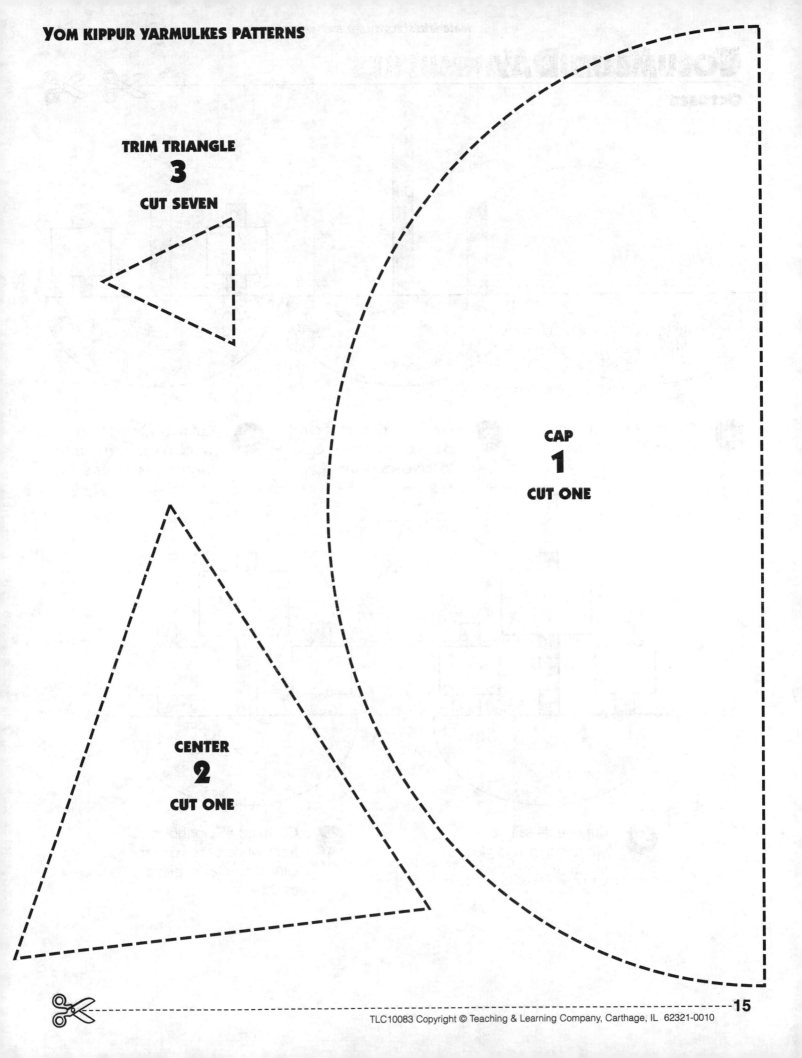

TRIM TRIANGLE
3
CUT SEVEN

CAP
1
CUT ONE

CENTER
2
CUT ONE

COLUMBUS DAY
OCTOBER

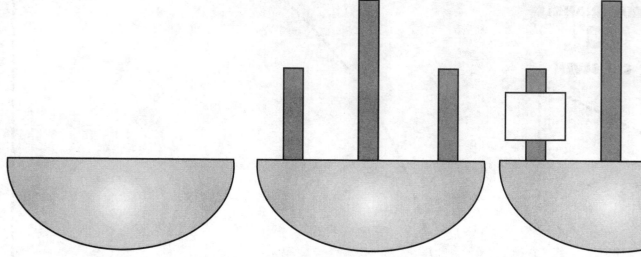

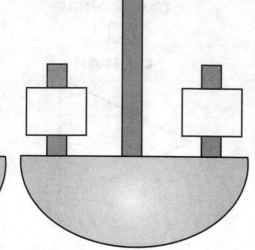

1 Cut one #1 boat from brown or tan paper.

2 Cut three #2 masts from dark brown paper. Glue to the back of the boat as shown.

3 Cut two #3 sails from white paper and glue to the two outer masts.

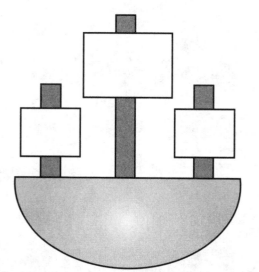

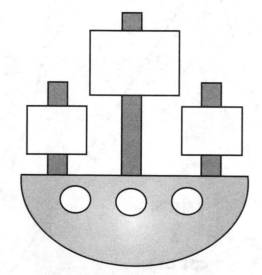

4 Cut one #4 sail from white paper and glue to the middle mast as shown.

5 Cut three #5 portholes from white or tan paper. Glue the holes in place as shown.

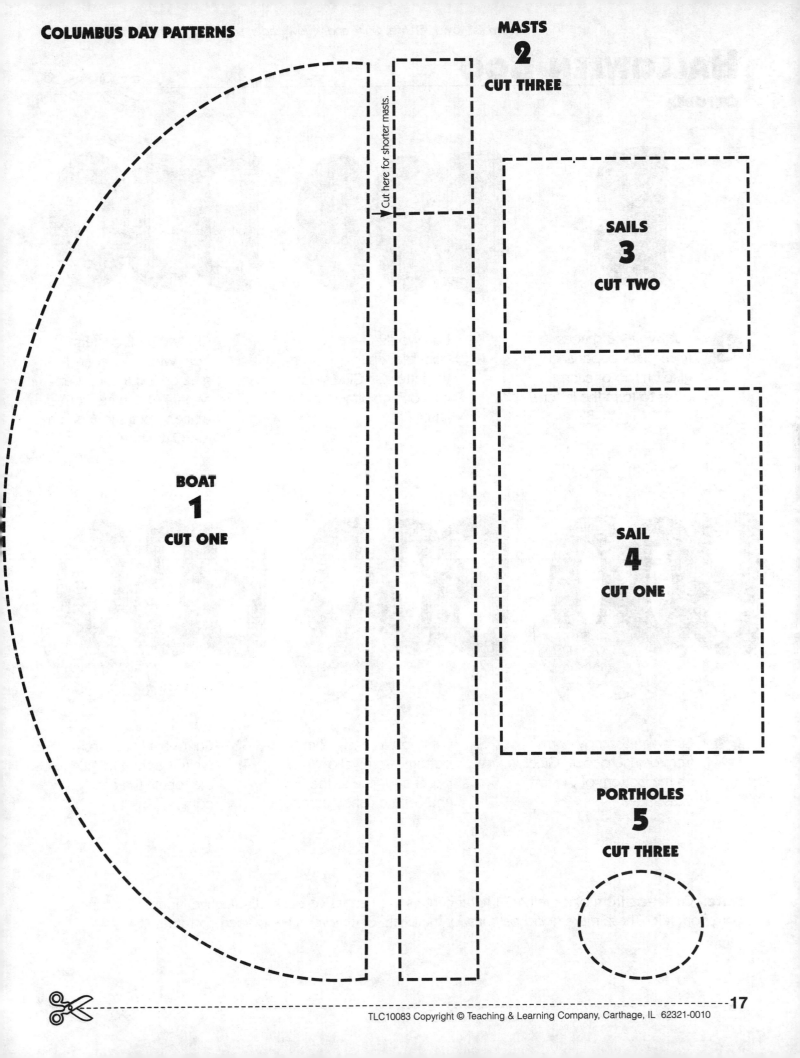

COLUMBUS DAY PATTERNS

MASTS
2
CUT THREE

Cut here for shorter masts.

SAILS
3
CUT TWO

BOAT
1
CUT ONE

SAIL
4
CUT ONE

PORTHOLES
5
CUT THREE

Materials: *black, orange, white and yellow paper; scissors; glue; black crayon or marker*

Halloween Boo

October

1 Cut two #1 B shapes from black paper and glue on top of each other to form the letter *B*.

2 Cut two #2 O shapes from black paper to form the letter *O*. Glue side by side and attach to the letter *B*.

3 Cut two #3 B centers from white paper and glue on the *B* part. Cut two #4 O centers from white paper and glue on the *O* as shown.

4 Cut two #5 candy corns from orange paper. Glue on the bottom of the last *O* as shown.

5 Cut two #6 candy corn bottoms from yellow paper and glue to the ends of the candy corn.

6 Cut two #7 tops from white paper and glue to the top of the candy corn.

Note: Cut letters from black felt. Cut letter centers from adhesive-backed reflective fabric. Cut candy corn from felt. These make good patches for the backs of children's Halloween costumes.

HALLOWEEN BOO PATTERNS

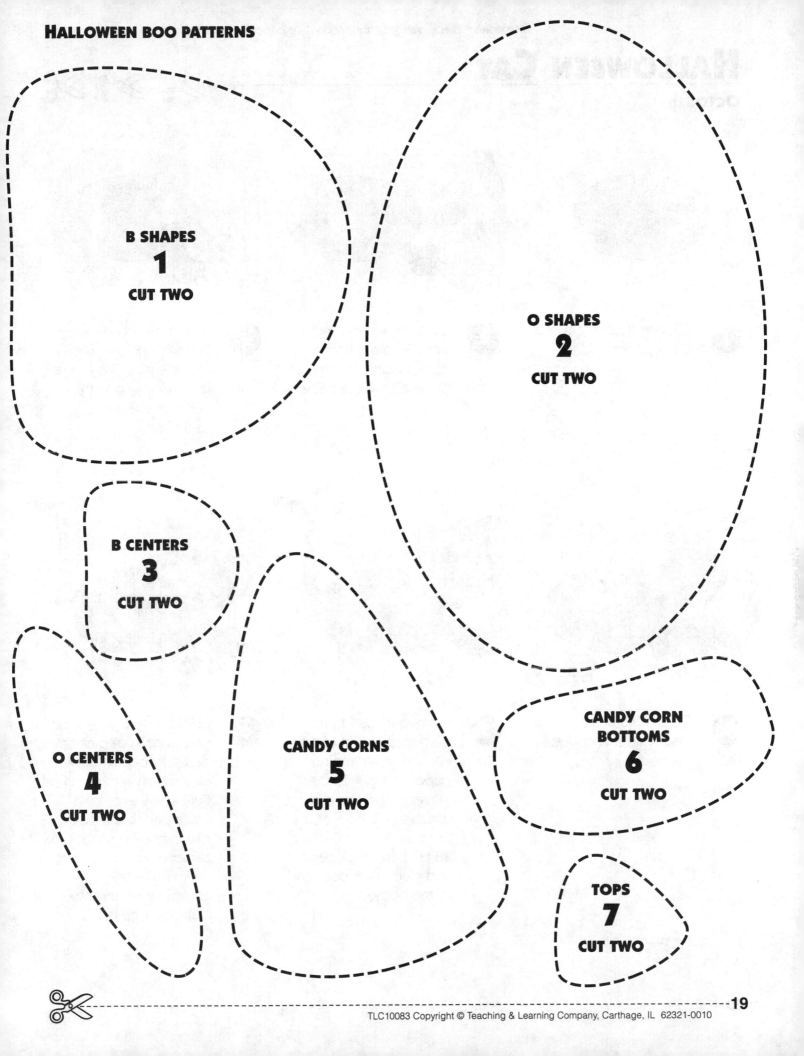

B SHAPES
1
CUT TWO

O SHAPES
2
CUT TWO

B CENTERS
3
CUT TWO

O CENTERS
4
CUT TWO

CANDY CORNS
5
CUT TWO

CANDY CORN BOTTOMS
6
CUT TWO

TOPS
7
CUT TWO

HALLOWEEN CAT

OCTOBER

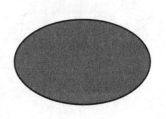

1 Cut one #1 body from black paper.

2 Cut three #2 legs and three #3 paws from black paper. Cut nine #4 claws from black paper.

3 Glue the legs on the body as shown. Then glue the #3 paws to the legs. Finally, glue three claws to the back of each paw.

4 Cut one #5 head from black paper and glue to the body.

5 Cut two #6 ears from black paper. Cut two #7 ear centers from pink paper and glue to the center of the ears and attach to the back of the head as shown. Cut one #8 tail from black paper and glue to the back end of the body.

6 Cut a tiny triangle for the cat's nose from pink or dark gray paper. Draw on a mouth with a marker. Cut two #9 eyes from white paper. Cut two #10 pupils from black paper. Glue in place as shown. (Note: You could use a marker to make the pupils.)

HALLOWEEN CAT PATTERNS

BODY
1
CUT ONE

LEGS
2
CUT THREE

CLAWS
4
CUT NINE

PAWS
3
CUT THREE

Note:
Glue the cat head, paws and tail to the top of a small brown paper lunch sack to make a puppet or treat bag.

Halloween Cat Patterns

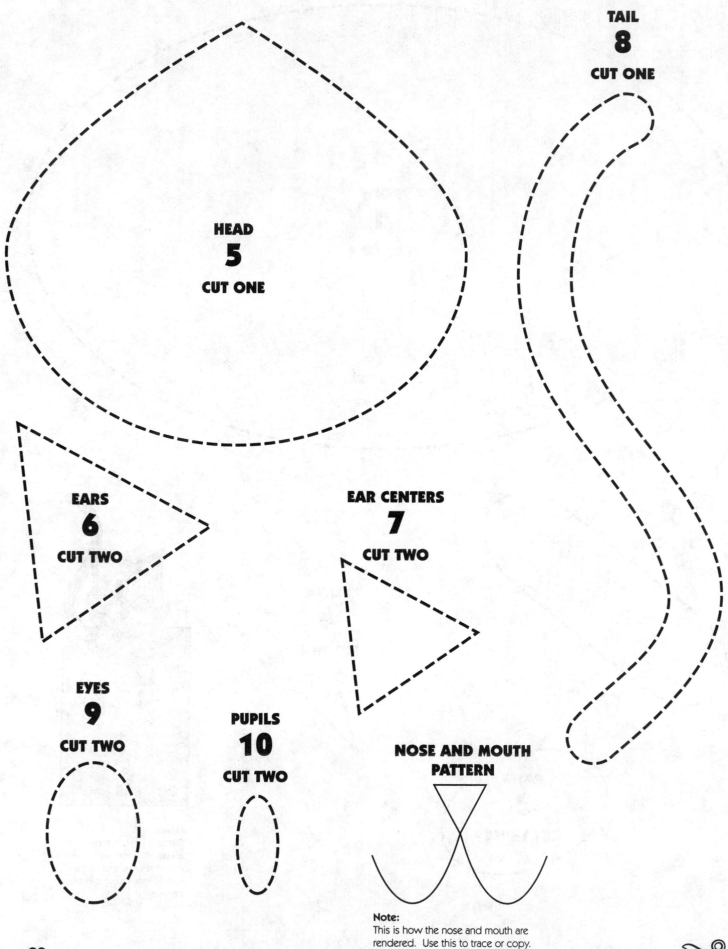

TAIL
8
CUT ONE

HEAD
5
CUT ONE

EARS
6
CUT TWO

EAR CENTERS
7
CUT TWO

EYES
9
CUT TWO

PUPILS
10
CUT TWO

NOSE AND MOUTH PATTERN

Note:
This is how the nose and mouth are rendered. Use this to trace or copy.

Materials: *black, orange, white and yellow paper; scissors; glue; black crayon or marker*

ALLOWEEN PUMPKI

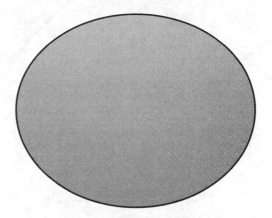

1 Cut one #1 pumpkin from orange paper.

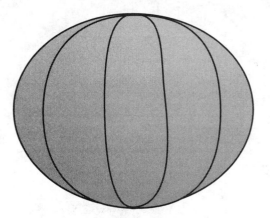

2 Use a marker to draw lines on the pumpkin as shown.

3 Cut the shapes you want to use for the mouth, nose and eyes. Glue in place.

4 Cut one #2 stem from brown paper and glue to the back at the top of the pumpkin. (Note: A tooth and pupils have been added out of white paper to finish the pumpkin.)

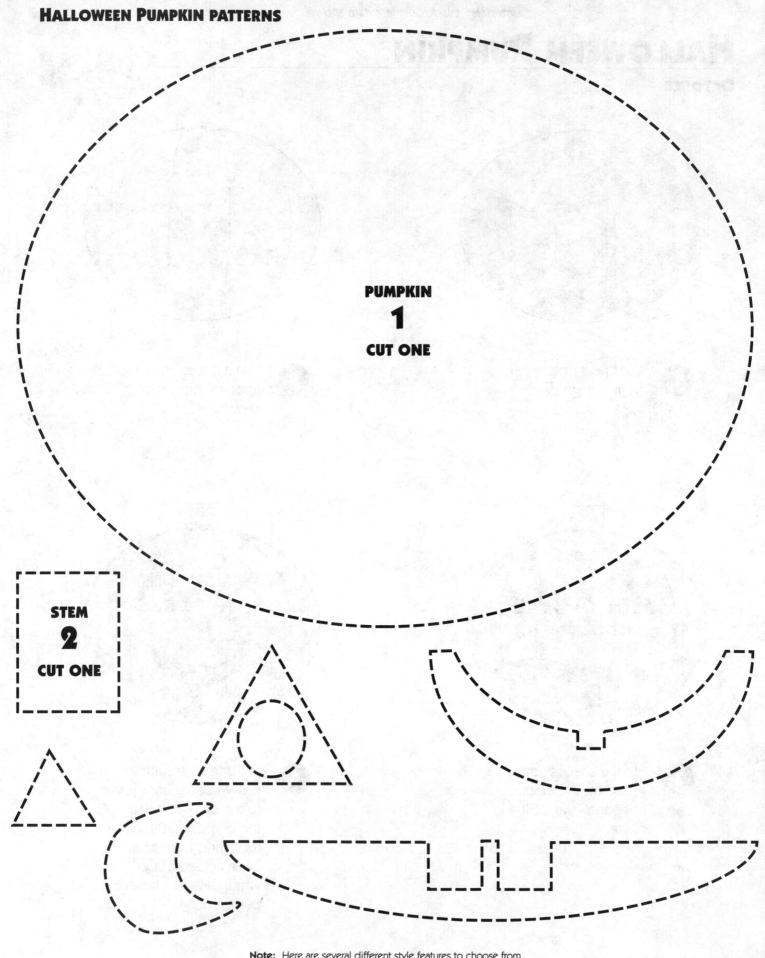

PUMPKIN
1
CUT ONE

STEM
2
CUT ONE

Note: Here are several different style features to choose from.

Materials: black, brown, gray, tan and white paper; scissors; glue; black crayon or marker

ELECTION DAY

NOVEMBER

1 Cut two #1 heads, one from gray paper and one from brown paper.

2 Cut two #2 ears from brown paper. Cut two #3 ear centers from tan or white paper. Glue the ear centers on top of the ears. Then glue to back of the brown head.

3 Glue the gray #1 head to the side of the brown head as shown.

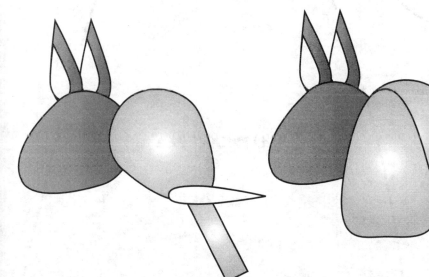
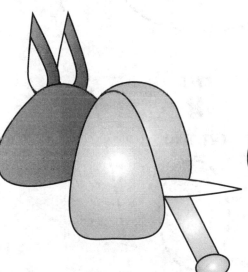

4 Cut one #4 tusk from white paper and glue to the bottom of the gray head. Cut one #5 trunk from gray paper. Glue to the bottom of the gray head.

5 Cut one #6 nose from gray paper and glue to the bottom of the elephant's trunk. Cut one #7 ear from gray paper and glue in place as shown.

6 Cut two #8 eyes from white paper and glue in place as shown. Cut five #9 pupils and nostrils and glue as shown. Add the donkey's smile using black crayon or marker.

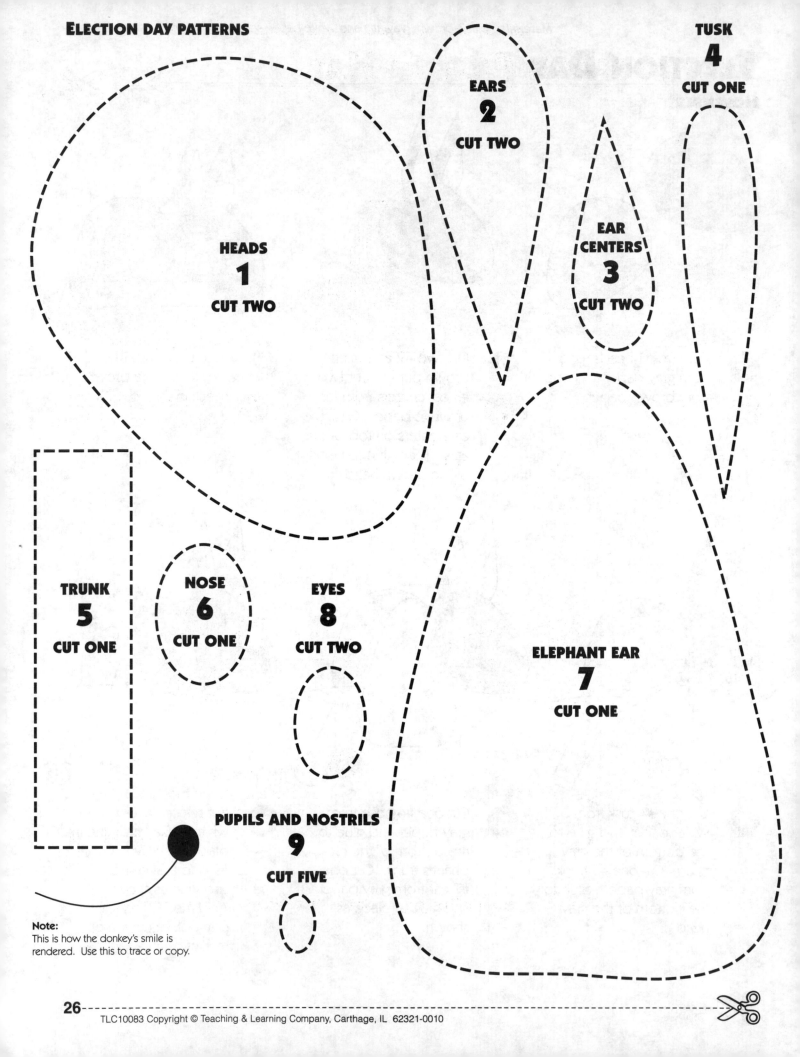

ELECTION DAY PATTERNS

TUSK
4
CUT ONE

EARS
2
CUT TWO

EAR
CENTERS
3
CUT TWO

HEADS
1
CUT TWO

TRUNK
5
CUT ONE

NOSE
6
CUT ONE

EYES
8
CUT TWO

ELEPHANT EAR
7
CUT ONE

PUPILS AND NOSTRILS
9
CUT FIVE

Note:
This is how the donkey's smile is rendered. Use this to trace or copy.

Materials: *black, brown, gold and white paper; scissors; glue; black crayon or marker*

THA KSGIVING PILGRIM HAT

NOVEMBER

1 Cut one #1 brim from brown paper.

2 Cut one #2 hat from brown paper and glue to the middle of the brim as shown.

3 Cut one #3 band from gold or white paper and glue to the bottom of the hat.

4 Cut one #4 buckle from black paper and glue to the bottom center of the band.

5 Cut one #5 buckle center from gold or white paper and glue in the middle of the buckle.

Note: These hats make great place cards for Thanksgiving dinner. Write each guest's name on the hat, above the buckle.

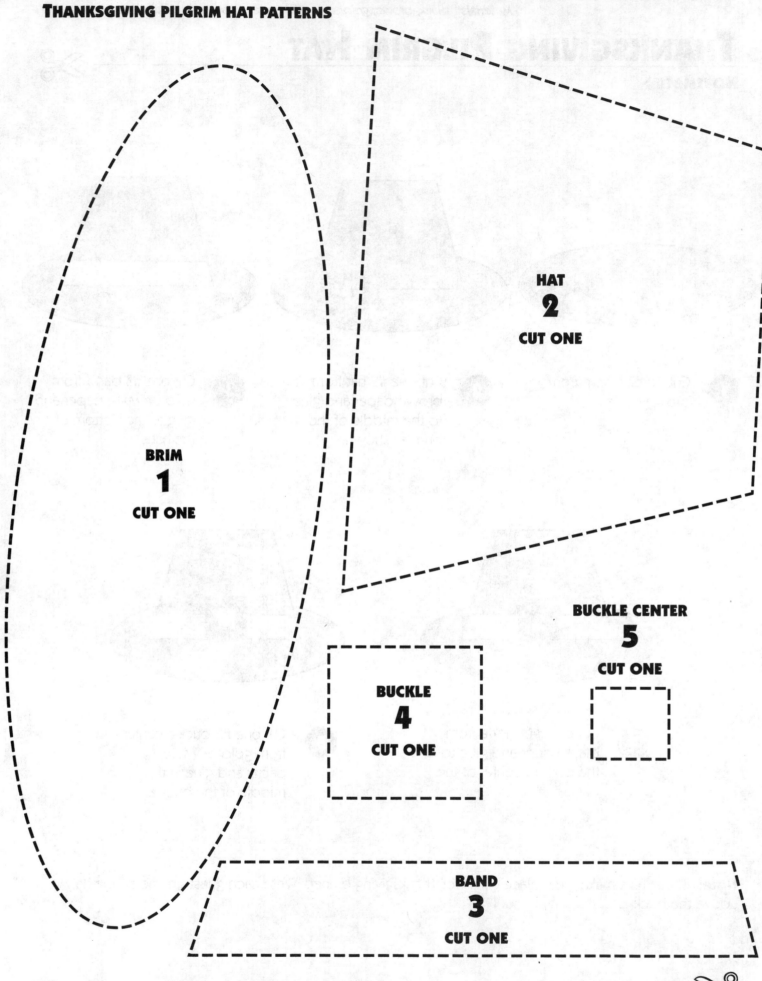

BRIM
1
CUT ONE

HAT
2
CUT ONE

BUCKLE CENTER
5
CUT ONE

BUCKLE
4
CUT ONE

BAND
3
CUT ONE

THANKSGIVING TURKEY

NOVEMBER

1 Cut one #1 body from brown paper. Cut six #2 feathers from a variety of fall colors. Glue to the underside of the top half of the body.

2 Cut three #3 feathers from a variety of fall colors. Glue to the underside of the bottom half of the body.

3 Cut three #4 wing feathers from a variety of fall colors. Glue to the middle of the body as shown.

4 Cut one #5 wing from brown paper and glue over the top of the wing feathers.

5 Cut one #6 head from brown paper and glue in place. Cut two #7 legs from yellow paper and glue to the underside of the bottom of the body. Cut two #8 feet and glue to the legs as shown.

6 Cut two #9 wattles from red paper and glue to the bottom of the head. Cut one #10 beak from yellow paper and glue to the underside of the head. Cut one #11 eye from black paper and glue in place.

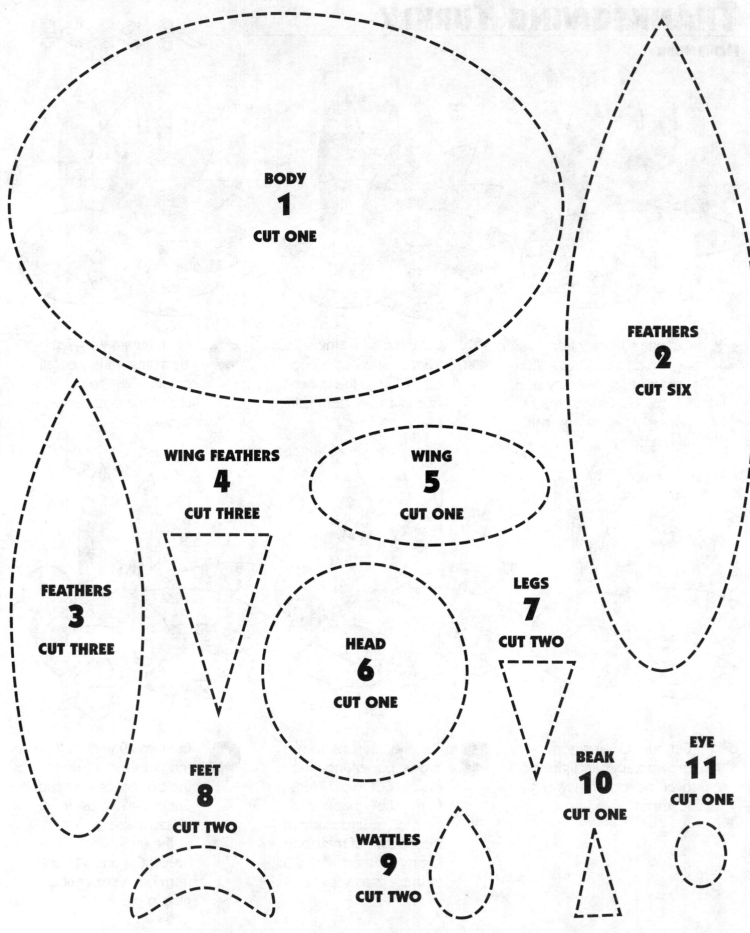

BODY
1
CUT ONE

FEATHERS
2
CUT SIX

WING FEATHERS
4
CUT THREE

WING
5
CUT ONE

FEATHERS
3
CUT THREE

HEAD
6
CUT ONE

LEGS
7
CUT TWO

FEET
8
CUT TWO

WATTLES
9
CUT TWO

BEAK
10
CUT ONE

EYE
11
CUT ONE

Materials: *blue, red, white and yellow; scissors; glue; black crayon and marker*

HANUKKAH MENORAH

DECEMBER

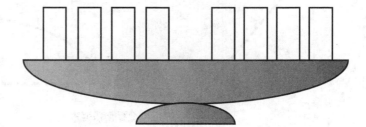

1 Cut one #1 candle holder and one #2 base from blue paper. Glue the base to the candle holder as shown.

2 Cut eight #3 candles from white paper. Four are glued to each side of the candle holder.

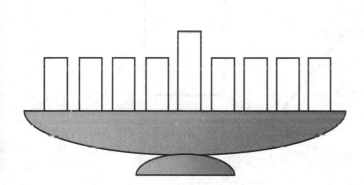

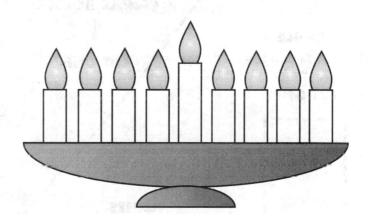

3 Cut one #4 candle from white paper and glue to the middle of the candle holder.

4 Cut nine #5 flames from yellow or red paper and glue to the back of each candle at the top.

Note: Outline each flame with glitter glue for a sparkling effect.

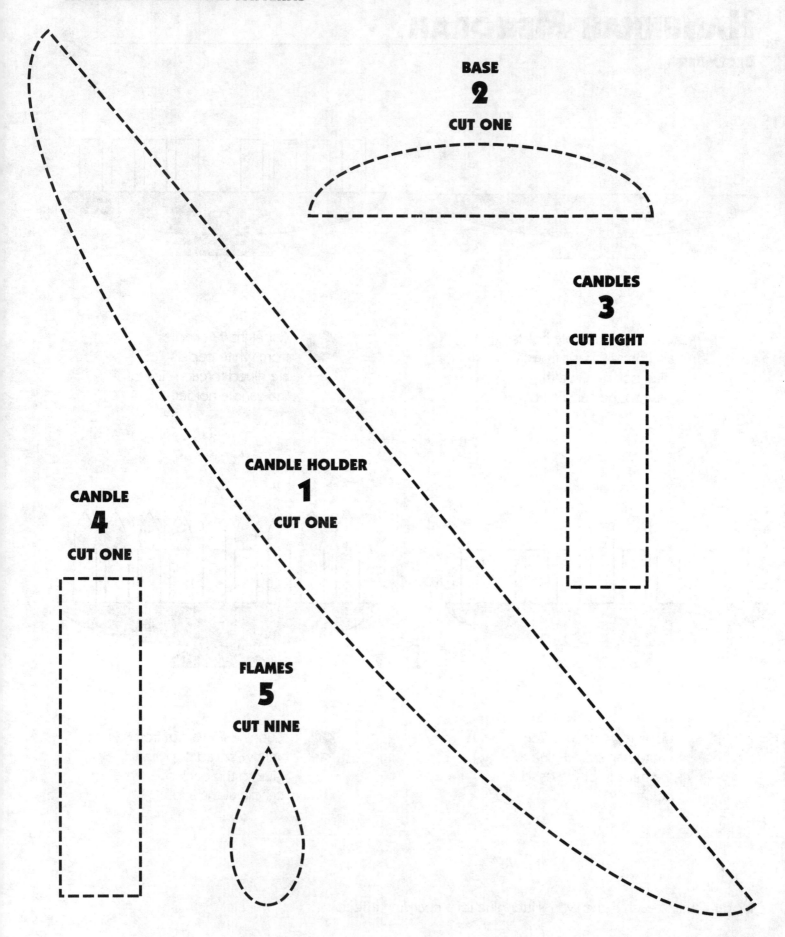

BASE

2

CUT ONE

CANDLES

3

CUT EIGHT

CANDLE HOLDER

1

CUT ONE

CANDLE

4

CUT ONE

FLAMES

5

CUT NINE

Materials: *green, red and yellow paper; scissors; glue*
Optional Materials: *gold sequins*

CHRISTMAS POINSETTIA

DECEMBER

1 Cut three #1 leaves from green paper and arrange them as shown.

2 Cut eight #2 petals from red paper. Start gluing them on top of the leaves in a circular pattern.

3 This is how your poinsettia should look.

4 Cut seven #3 centers from yellow paper and glue them randomly in the center of the poinsettia. (Note: You may use dots from a hole punch.)

Note: Gluing gold sequins in the center will make your flower more festive.

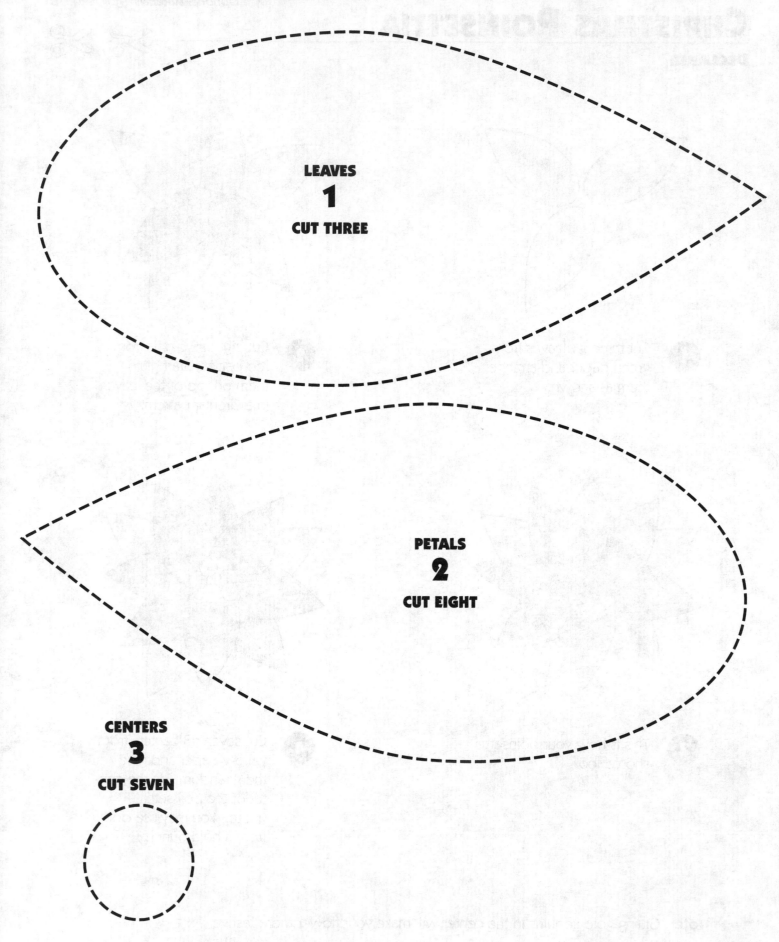

LEAVES
1
CUT THREE

PETALS
2
CUT EIGHT

CENTERS
3
CUT SEVEN

CHRISTMAS DEER

DECEMBER

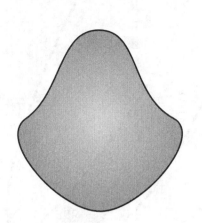 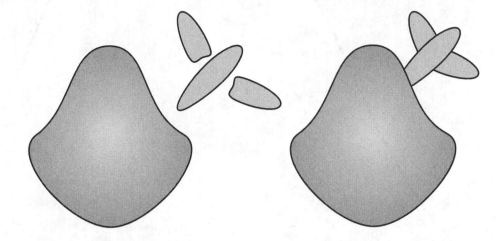

1 Cut one #1 head from brown paper.

2 Cut two #2 antler stems from tan paper. Cut four #3 antler branches from tan paper. These will make two sets of antlers.

3 Assemble them as shown.

4 Draw on a mouth with a marker.

5 Cut one #4 nose from red paper or use a marker to draw one.

6 Cut two #5 eyes from white paper and two #6 pupils from black paper and glue in place, or use a marker to draw in the pupils.

CHRISTMAS DEER PATTERNS

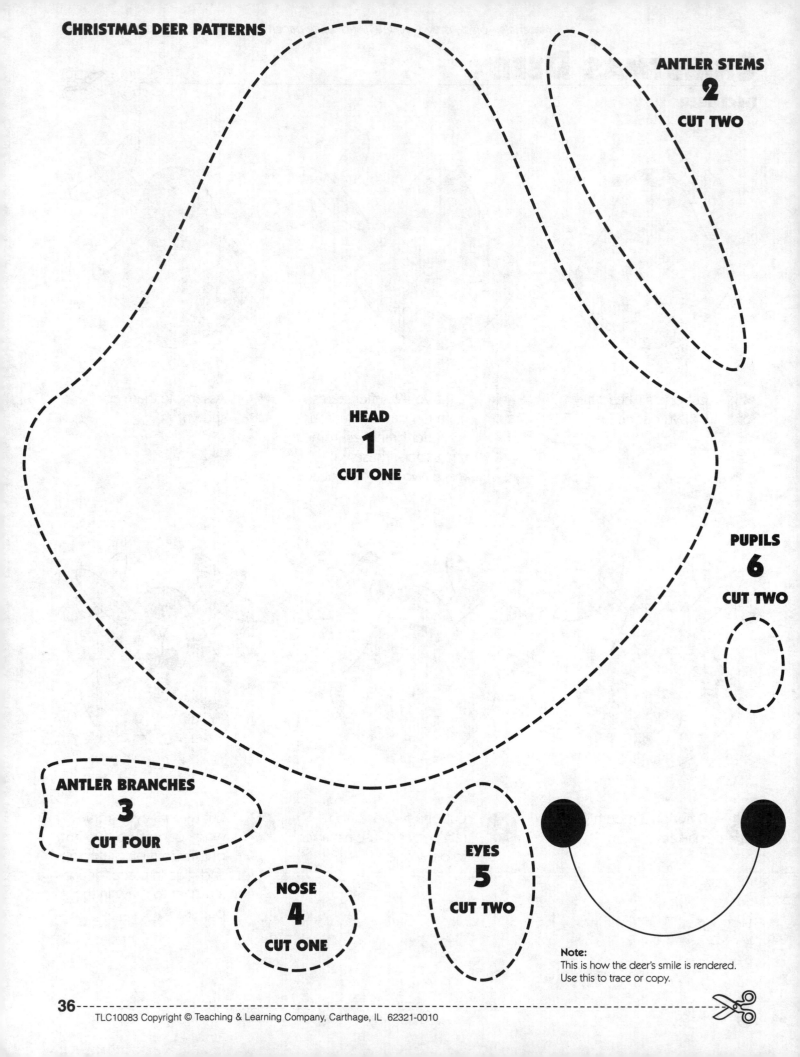

ANTLER STEMS
2
CUT TWO

HEAD
1
CUT ONE

PUPILS
6
CUT TWO

ANTLER BRANCHES
3
CUT FOUR

NOSE
4
CUT ONE

EYES
5
CUT TWO

Note:
This is how the deer's smile is rendered.
Use this to trace or copy.

Materials: black, green, pale pink, red and white paper; scissors; glue; black crayon or marker

CHRISTMAS SANTA

DECEMBER

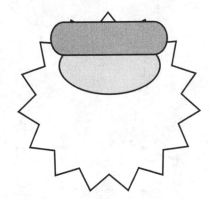

1 Cut one #1 beard from white paper.

2 Cut one #2 face from pale pink and glue to the upper half of the beard as shown.

3 Cut one #3 hat band from green paper and glue to the top part of the face.

4 Cut one #4 hat from red paper and glue to the back side of the hat band.

5 Cut two #5 mustaches from white paper and glue to the bottom of the face. Cut one #6 tassel from white paper and glue to the top of the hat.

6 Cut one #7 nose from red paper. Glue in place. Cut two #8 eyes from black paper or use a marker to make the eyes.

Note: Cut beard from poster board. Complete Santa as directed in steps 2-5. Attach nose. Glue craft stick onto the bottom of the beard. Poke eye holes with a pencil or nail and enlarge. Now Santa is a mask!

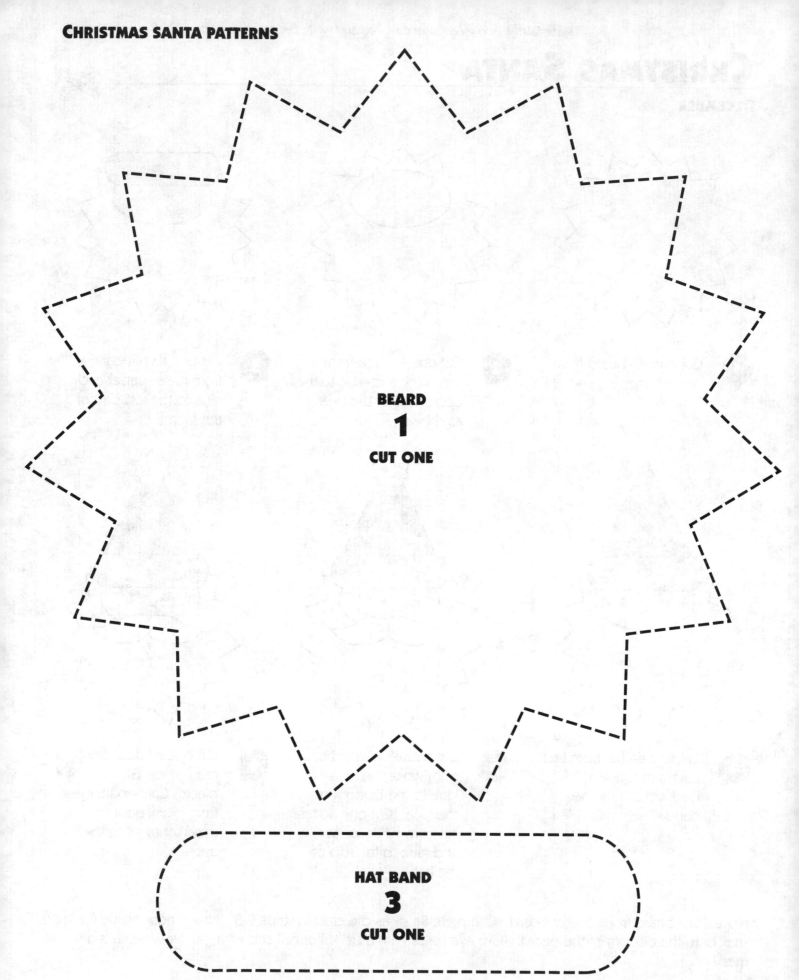

BEARD
1
CUT ONE

HAT BAND
3
CUT ONE

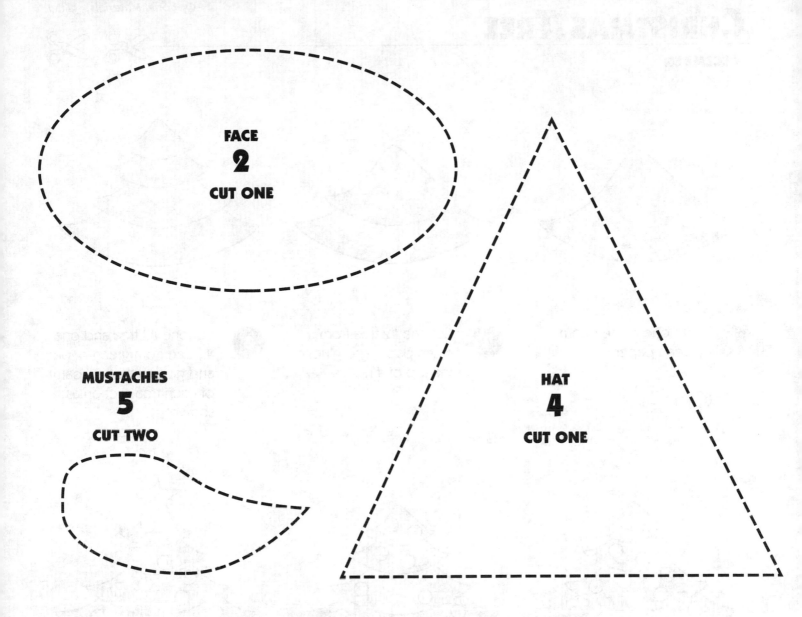

FACE
2
CUT ONE

MUSTACHES
5
CUT TWO

HAT
4
CUT ONE

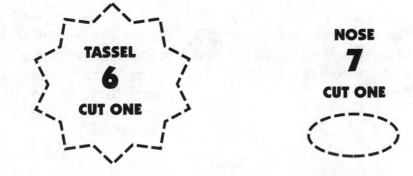

TASSEL
6
CUT ONE

NOSE
7
CUT ONE

EYES
8
CUT TWO

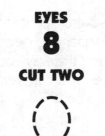

Materials: brown, gold, green and red paper; scissors; glue; black crayon or marker

Optional Materials: glitter

CHRISTMAS TREE

DECEMBER

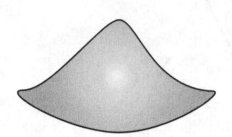

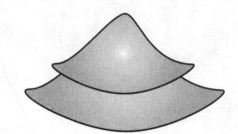

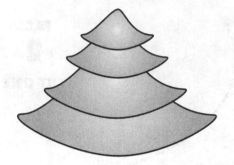

1 Cut one #1 tree from green paper.

2 Cut one #2 tree from green paper and glue to the top of #1.

3 Cut one #3 tree and one #4 tree from green paper and glue to the top part of each tree section as shown.

4 Cut several #5 balls from red paper and decorate the tree the way you like. (Note: You can use various colors.)

5 Cut one #6 trunk from brown paper and glue to the bottom of the tree.

6 Cut one #7 star from gold paper and glue at the top of the tree. (Note: Using glitter and sequins creates a special festive touch.)

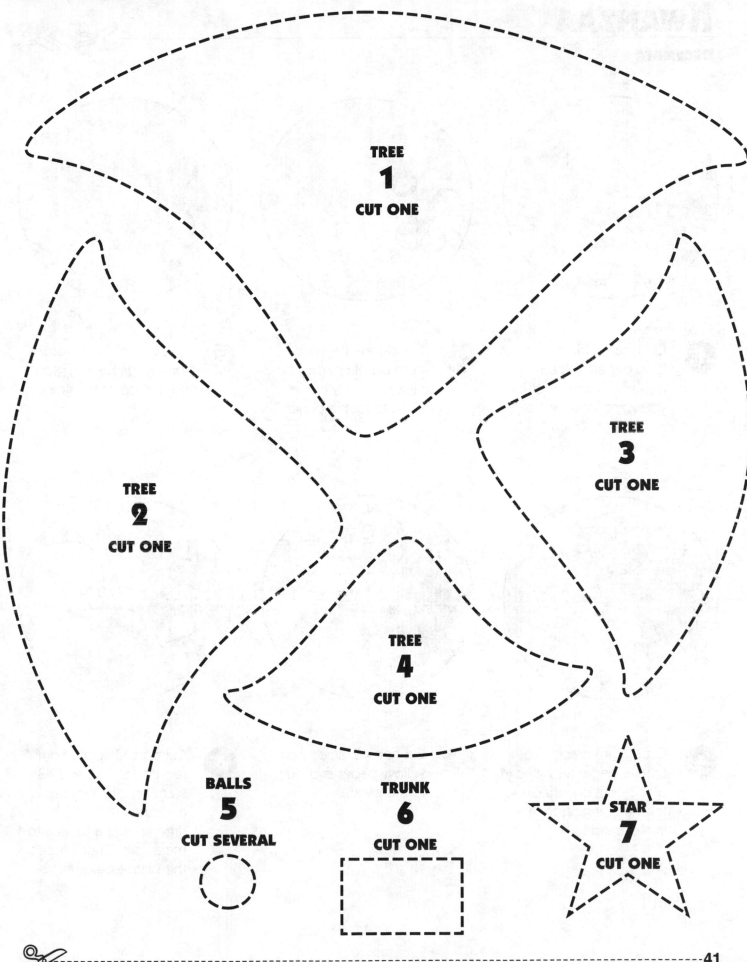

TREE
1
CUT ONE

TREE
2
CUT ONE

TREE
3
CUT ONE

TREE
4
CUT ONE

BALLS
5
CUT SEVERAL

TRUNK
6
CUT ONE

STAR
7
CUT ONE

Materials: *blue, brown, green, orange, purple, red, white and yellow paper; scissors; glue; black crayon or marker*

KWANZAA

DECEMBER

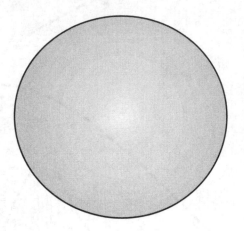

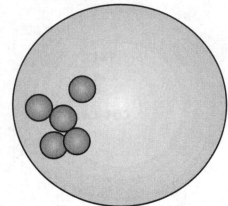

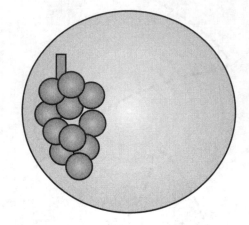

1 Cut one #1 plate from blue paper. (Note: You may use whatever color you want for the plate, or use a 6" [15 cm] paper plate.)

2 Cut eleven #2 grapes from purple paper and glue randomly to the plate to form a bunch.

3 Cut one #3 stem from brown paper and glue to the top of the grapes.

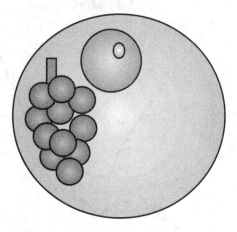

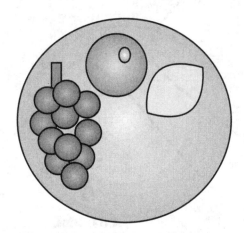

4 Cut one #4 orange from orange paper and glue in place. Cut one #5 circle for the orange from a lighter shade.

5 Cut one #6 lemon from yellow paper and glue to the plate.

6 Cut one #7 apple from red paper. Cut one #8 stem from brown paper and one #9 leaf from green paper and glue to the apple. Then glue to the plate as shown.

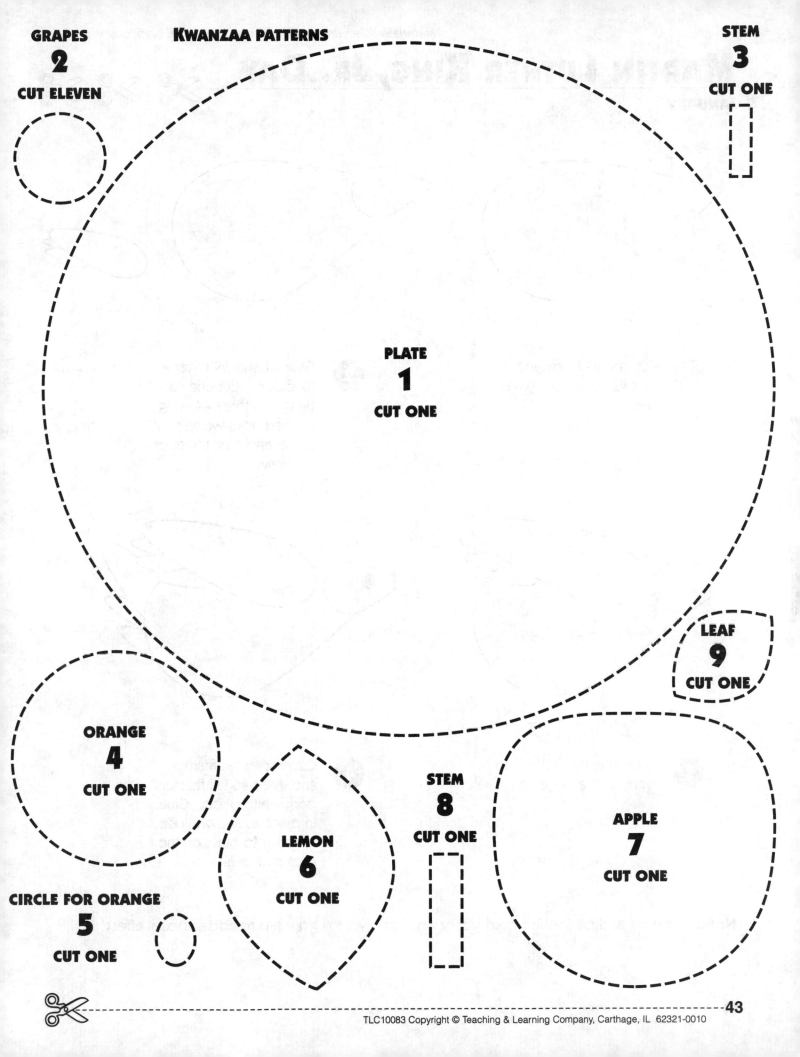

GRAPES

2

CUT ELEVEN

STEM

3

CUT ONE

PLATE

1

CUT ONE

LEAF

9

CUT ONE

ORANGE

4

CUT ONE

LEMON

6

CUT ONE

STEM

8

CUT ONE

APPLE

7

CUT ONE

CIRCLE FOR ORANGE

5

CUT ONE

MARTIN LUTHER KING, JR. DAY

JANUARY

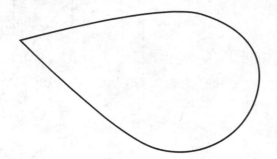

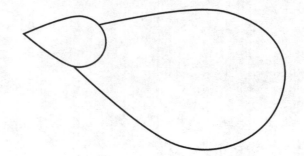

1 Cut one #1 body and one #2 head from white paper.

2 Glue #1 and #2 together as shown. Cut one #3 wing and three #4 wing feathers from white paper and glue together as shown.

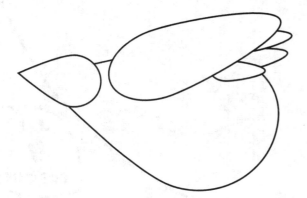

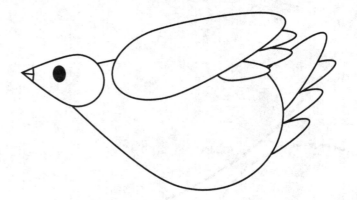

3 Then glue the feathers to body of the dove.

4 Cut one #5 tail feather and three #6 tail feathers from white paper. Glue in place as shown. Use a marker to draw on the eyes and beak.

Note: Cut wing and tail feathers from glossy white or silver foil gift wrap to add a special effect.

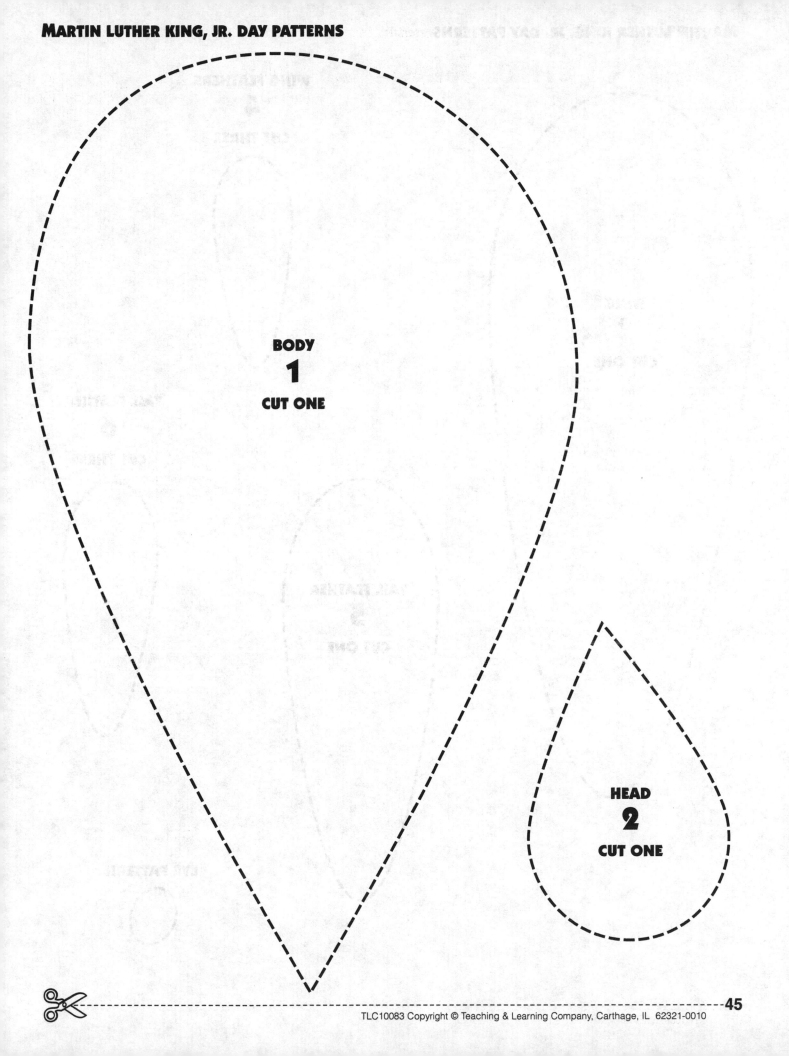

BODY
1
CUT ONE

HEAD
2
CUT ONE

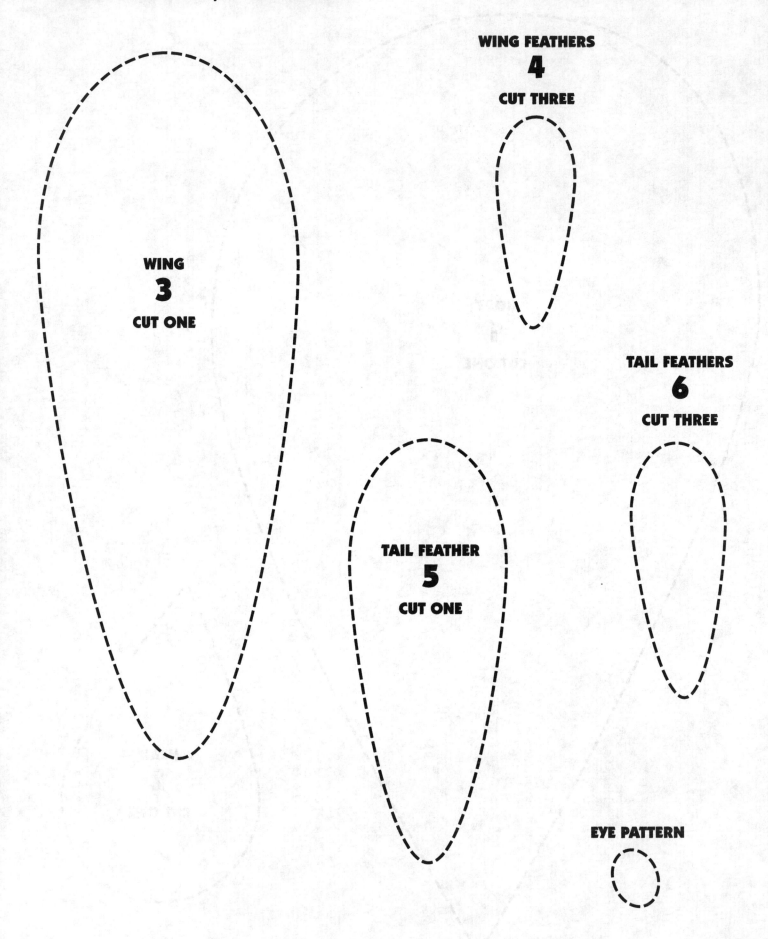

WING FEATHERS
4
CUT THREE

WING
3
CUT ONE

TAIL FEATHERS
6
CUT THREE

TAIL FEATHER
5
CUT ONE

EYE PATTERN

Materials: *black, brown, light gray, red and white paper; scissors; glue; black crayon and marker*

GROUNDHOG DAY
FEBRUARY

  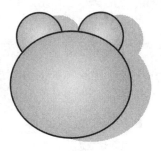

1 To make the shadow for the groundhog, cut one #1 head and two #2 ears from light gray paper. Glue in place as shown.

2 Cut two #2 ears from brown paper and glue slightly to the left side of the shadow ears.

3 Cut one #1 head from brown paper and glue slightly to the left side of the shadow head as shown.

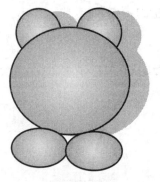

4 Cut two #3 feet from brown paper and glue to the bottom of the head.

5 Cut two #4 eyes from white paper. Use a marker to color the pupils in. Cut one #5 nose from black paper. Glue in place. Use a marker to draw on the mouth.

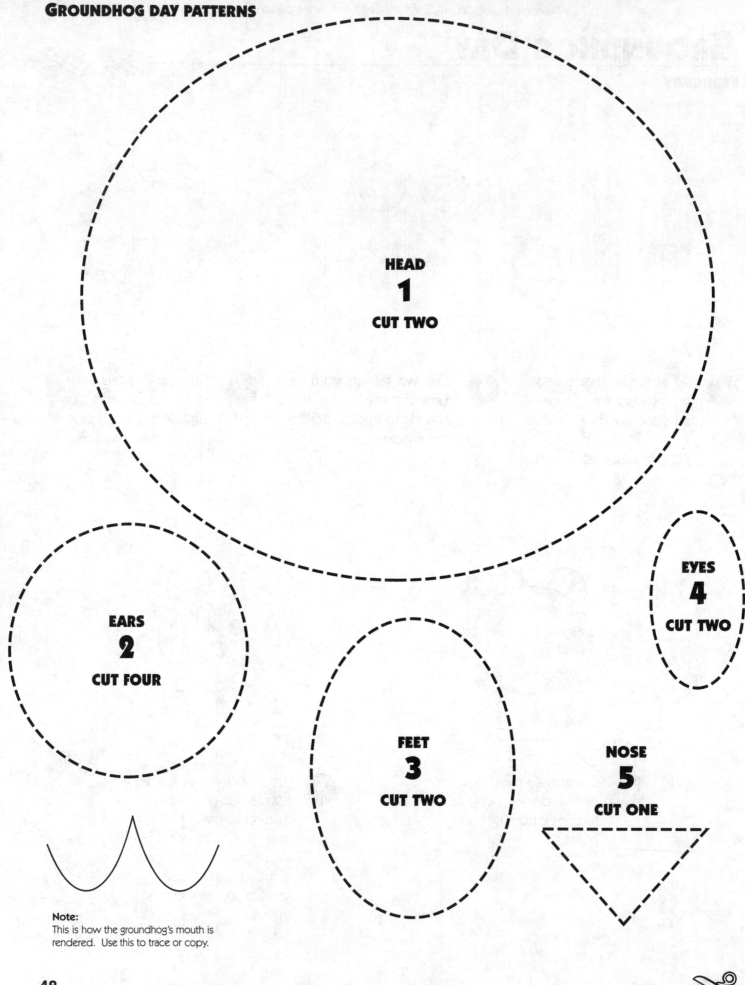

HEAD
1
CUT TWO

EYES
4
CUT TWO

EARS
2
CUT FOUR

FEET
3
CUT TWO

NOSE
5
CUT ONE

Note:
This is how the groundhog's mouth is
rendered. Use this to trace or copy.

VALENTINE BEAR
FEBRUARY

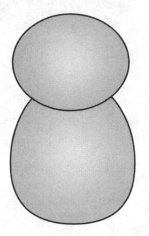

1 Cut one #1 body and one #2 head from brown paper. Glue together as shown.

2 Cut two #3 ears from brown paper. Cut two #4 ear centers from tan paper. Glue the #4 centers on the #3 ears and glue to the head as shown.

3 Cut two #5 arms and two #6 legs from brown paper. Glue the arms and legs to the sides of the body as shown.

4 Cut one #7 muzzle from light tan paper. Glue to the bottom half of the head. Cut one #8 heart from red paper. Glue on the body as shown.

5 Cut two #9 and two #10 arm and leg paw prints from black paper or use a marker to draw them. Glue in place.

6 Cut two #11 eyes from white paper. Use a marker to color the pupils in. Draw on a mouth and nose with a marker.

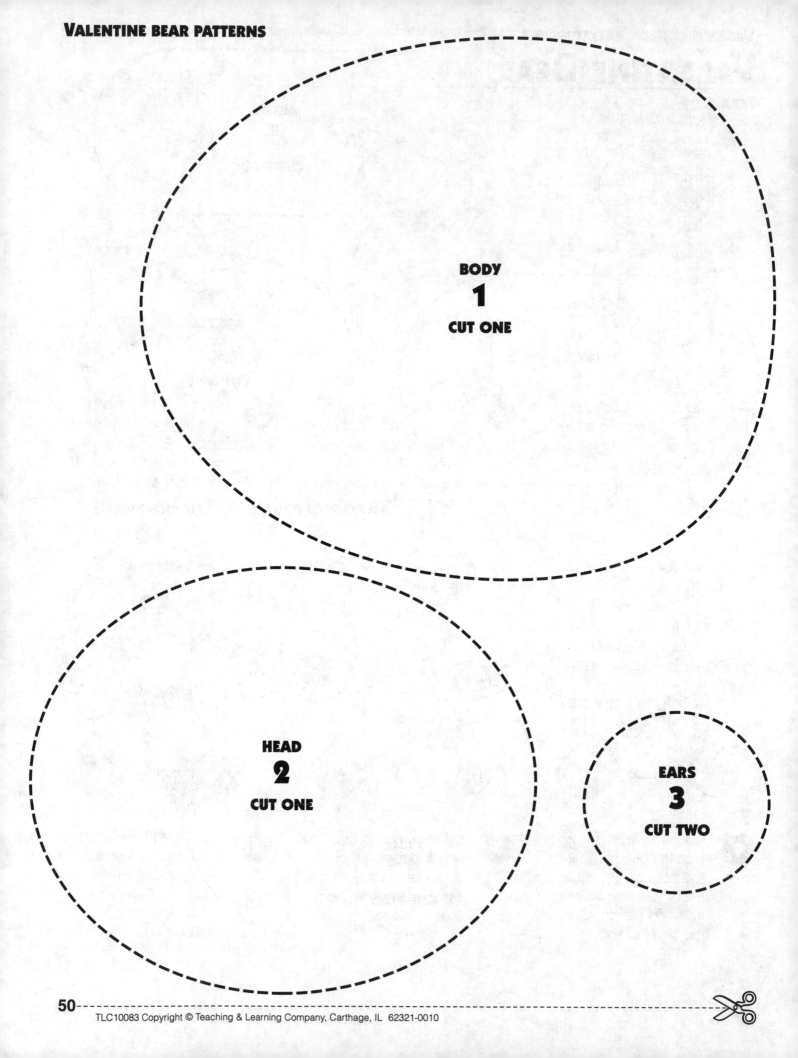

BODY
1
CUT ONE

HEAD
2
CUT ONE

EARS
3
CUT TWO

Valentine Bear Patterns

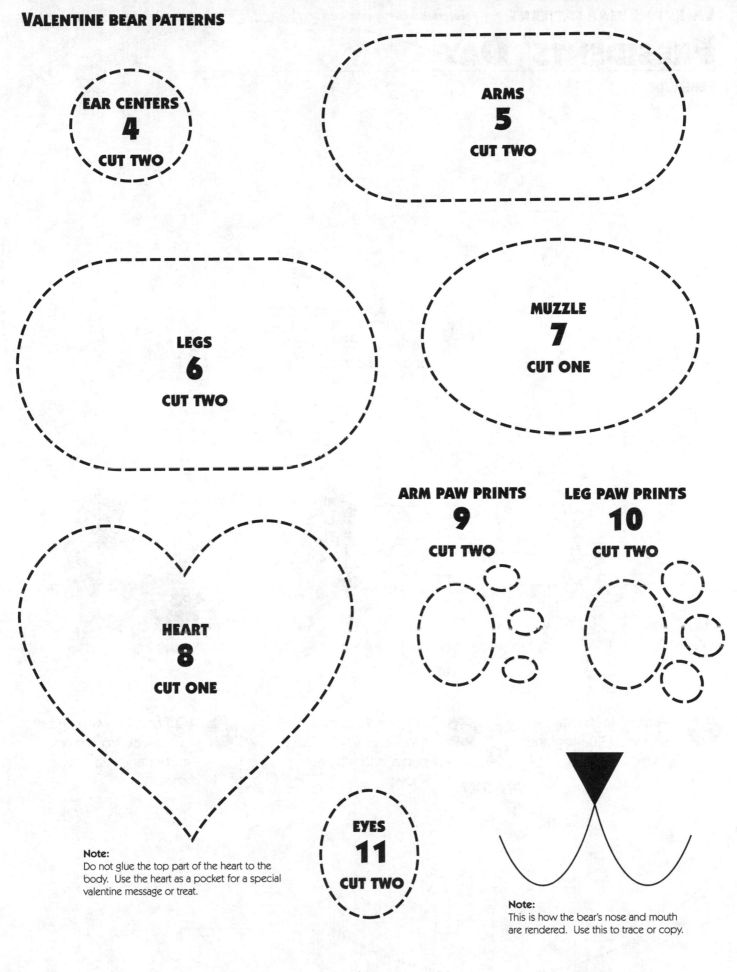

EAR CENTERS
4
CUT TWO

ARMS
5
CUT TWO

LEGS
6
CUT TWO

MUZZLE
7
CUT ONE

HEART
8
CUT ONE

ARM PAW PRINTS
9
CUT TWO

LEG PAW PRINTS
10
CUT TWO

EYES
11
CUT TWO

Note:
Do not glue the top part of the heart to the body. Use the heart as a pocket for a special valentine message or treat.

Note:
This is how the bear's nose and mouth are rendered. Use this to trace or copy.

PRESIDENTS' DAY

FEBRUARY

1 Cut three #1 stars one each from white, red and blue paper.

2 Assemble the stars as shown. Glue together.

3 Cut one #2 Lincoln silhouette from black paper and glue as shown.

4 Cut one #3 Washington silhouette from black paper and glue as shown.

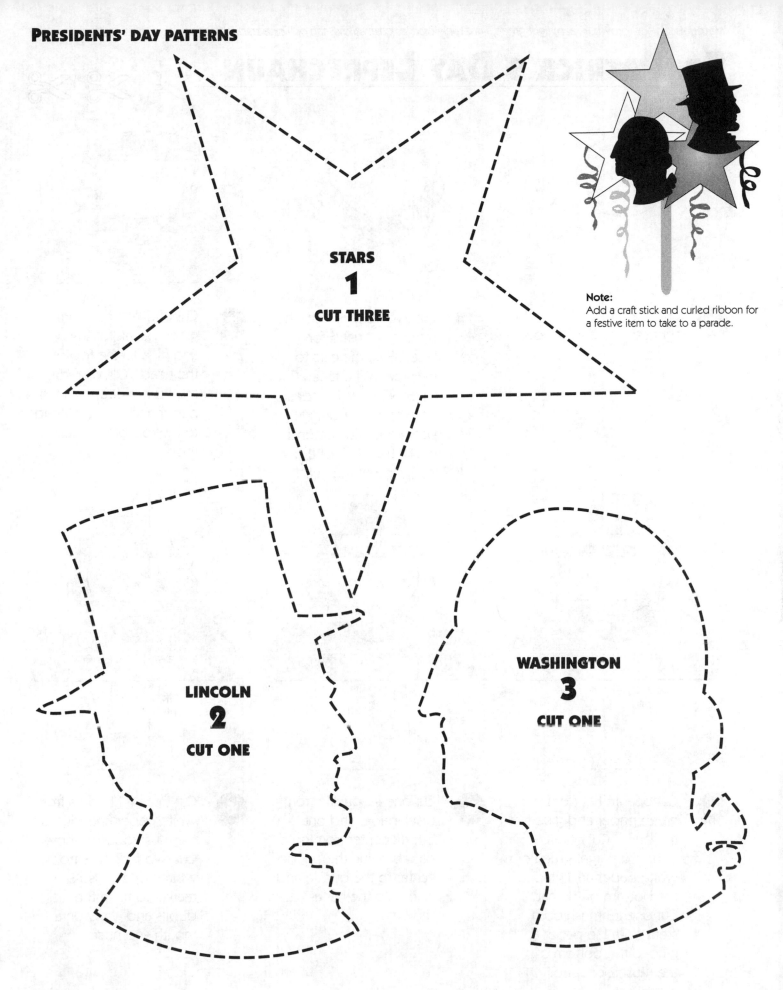

STARS

1

CUT THREE

Note:
Add a craft stick and curled ribbon for a festive item to take to a parade.

LINCOLN

2

CUT ONE

WASHINGTON

3

CUT ONE

St. Patrick's Day Leprechaun

MARCH

1 Cut one #1 head from light pink or pale yellow paper.

2 Cut two #2 ears from the same color used for face. Glue the ears to the side of the face. Cut seven #3 beard shapes from brown or orange paper and glue around the bottom half of the back side of the head.

3 Cut one #4 brim from green paper for the hat and glue to the top of the head. Cut one #5 mushroom cap from tan paper and glue the head to the top of the mushroom.

4 Cut one #6 hat from green paper and glue to the brim. Cut one #7 band from light green or white paper and glue to the bottom of the hat. Cut one #8 mushroom stem from tan paper and glue to the bottom of the mushroom cap.

5 Cut one #9 buckle from black paper and one #10 buckle center from gold paper. Glue the buckle center to the buckle and glue onto the hat as shown.

6 Cut three #11 spots from white paper and glue on the mushroom as shown. Cut two #12 eyes from white paper. Use a marker to fill in the pupils and draw on a mouth and nose.

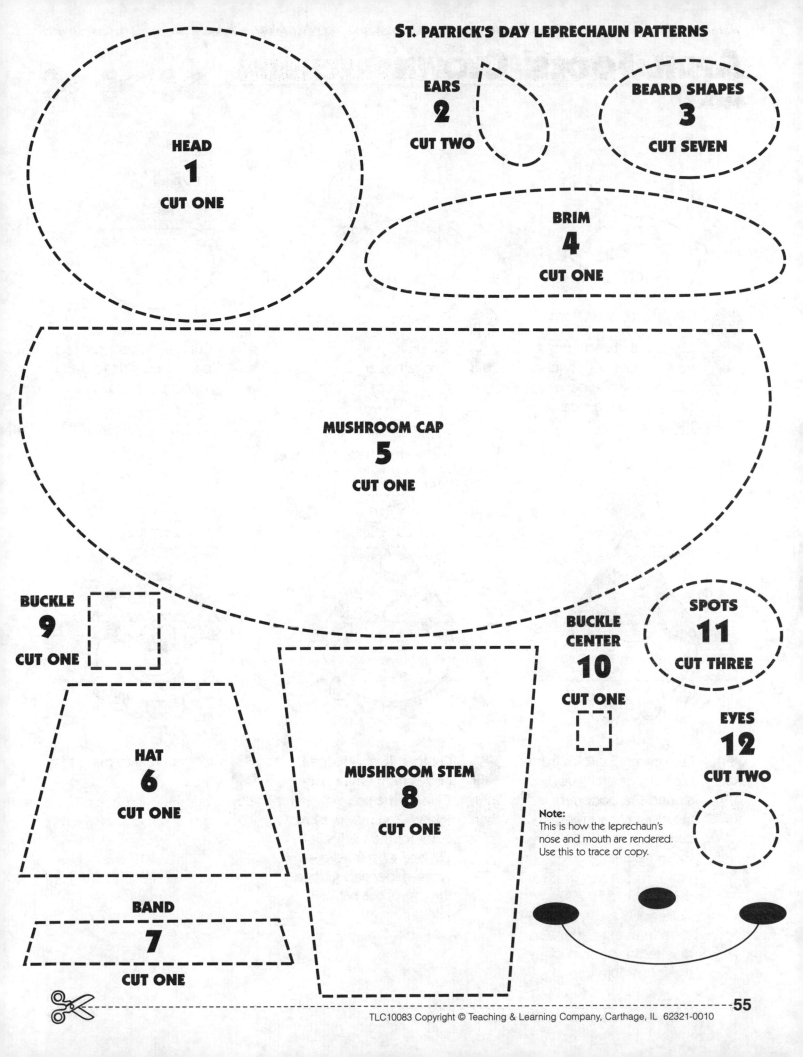

St. Patrick's Day Leprechaun Patterns

EARS
2
CUT TWO

BEARD SHAPES
3
CUT SEVEN

HEAD
1
CUT ONE

BRIM
4
CUT ONE

MUSHROOM CAP
5
CUT ONE

BUCKLE
9
CUT ONE

BUCKLE CENTER
10
CUT ONE

SPOTS
11
CUT THREE

HAT
6
CUT ONE

MUSHROOM STEM
8
CUT ONE

EYES
12
CUT TWO

BAND
7
CUT ONE

Note:
This is how the leprechaun's nose and mouth are rendered. Use this to trace or copy.

APRIL FOOLS' CLOW

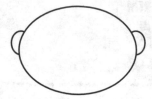

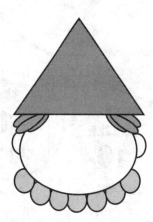

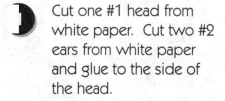

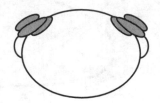

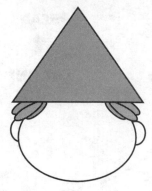

1 Cut one #1 head from white paper. Cut two #2 ears from white paper and glue to the side of the head.

2 Cut six #3 hair from orange paper. Glue three pieces to each side as shown.

3 Cut one #4 hat from red paper and glue to the top of the head. (Note: You may use any color for the hat.)

4 Cut seven #5 circles from blue paper and glue around the bottom of the clown head for the collar.

5 Cut four #5 and four #6 circles from white paper. Glue on the hat. (Note: You may use any color for the circles.) Cut one #7 star from white paper and glue to the top of the hat.

6 Use markers to make a face.

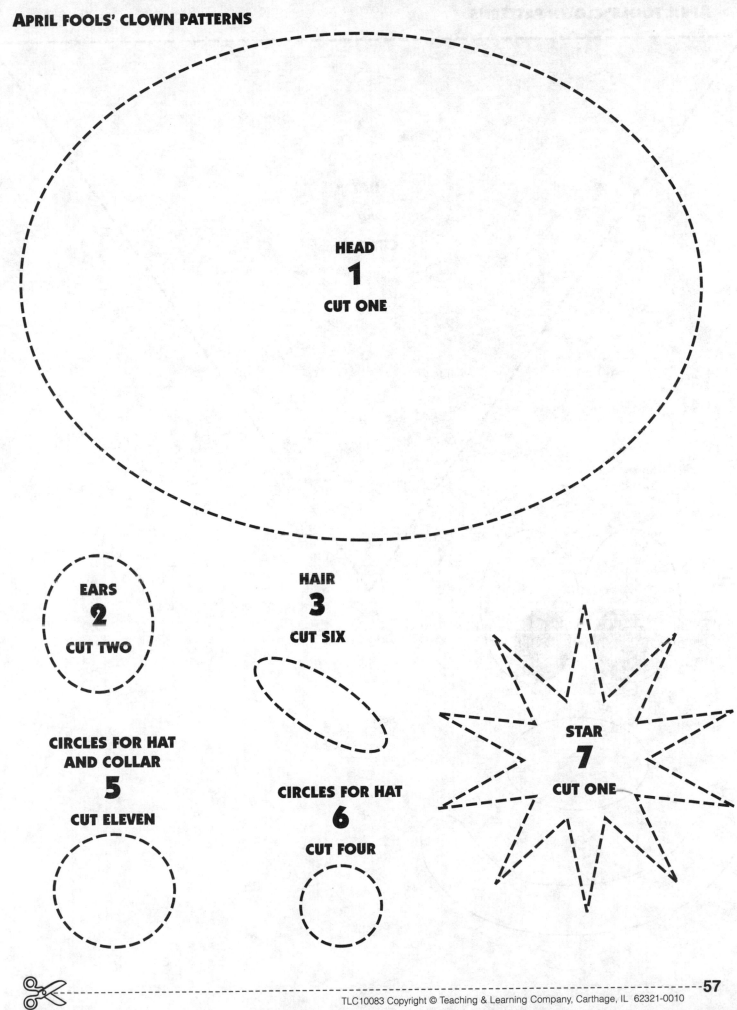

HEAD
1
CUT ONE

EARS
2
CUT TWO

HAIR
3
CUT SIX

CIRCLES FOR HAT AND COLLAR
5
CUT ELEVEN

CIRCLES FOR HAT
6
CUT FOUR

STAR
7
CUT ONE

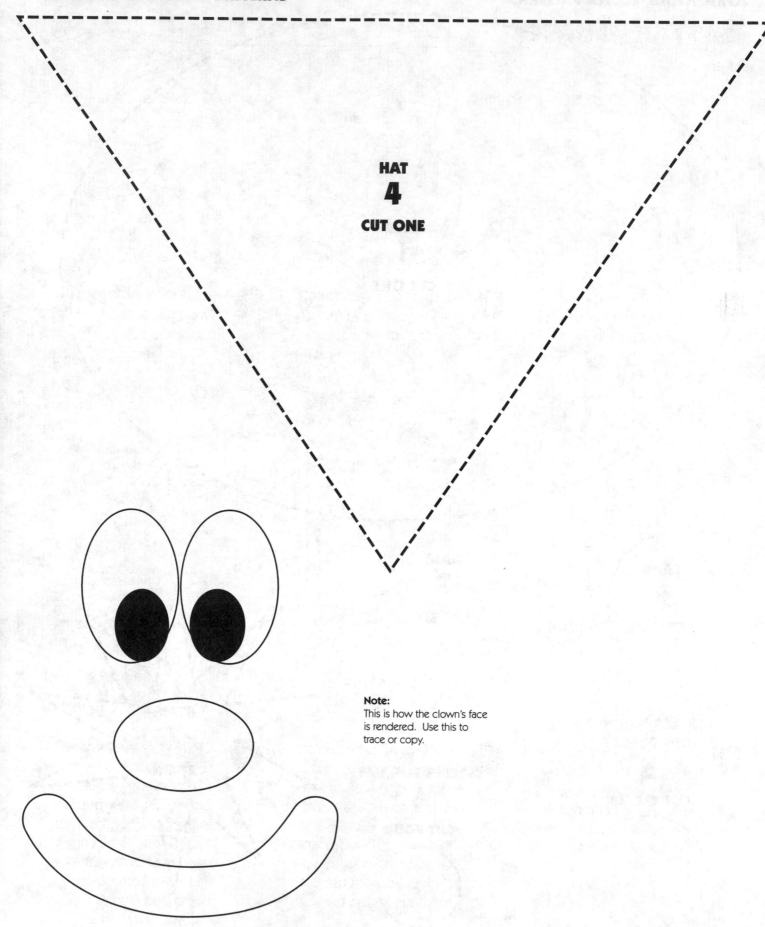

HAT
4
CUT ONE

Note:
This is how the clown's face
is rendered. Use this to
trace or copy.

Easter Bunny

April

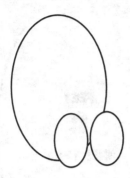

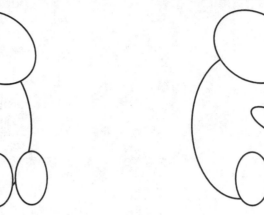

1 Cut one #1 body and two #2 feet from white paper and glue as shown.
(Note: You can make your bunny any color you want.)

2 Cut one #3 head from white paper and glue to the top of the body.

3 Cut two #4 arms from white paper and glue as shown.

4 Cut two #5 ears from white paper. Cut two #6 ears from pink paper and glue to the center of the #5 ears and attach to the back side of the head.

5 Cut two #7 paw prints from black paper and glue on the feet, or use a marker to make the feet paw prints. Cut several #8 tails from white paper. Glue on as shown.
(Note: You can use cotton balls for the tail.)

6 Cut two #9 eyes from white paper and two #10 pupils from black paper. Glue the pupils in the center of the eyes and glue on the bunny's head as shown. Cut one #11 nose from black paper and glue as shown. Draw on a mouth with a marker.

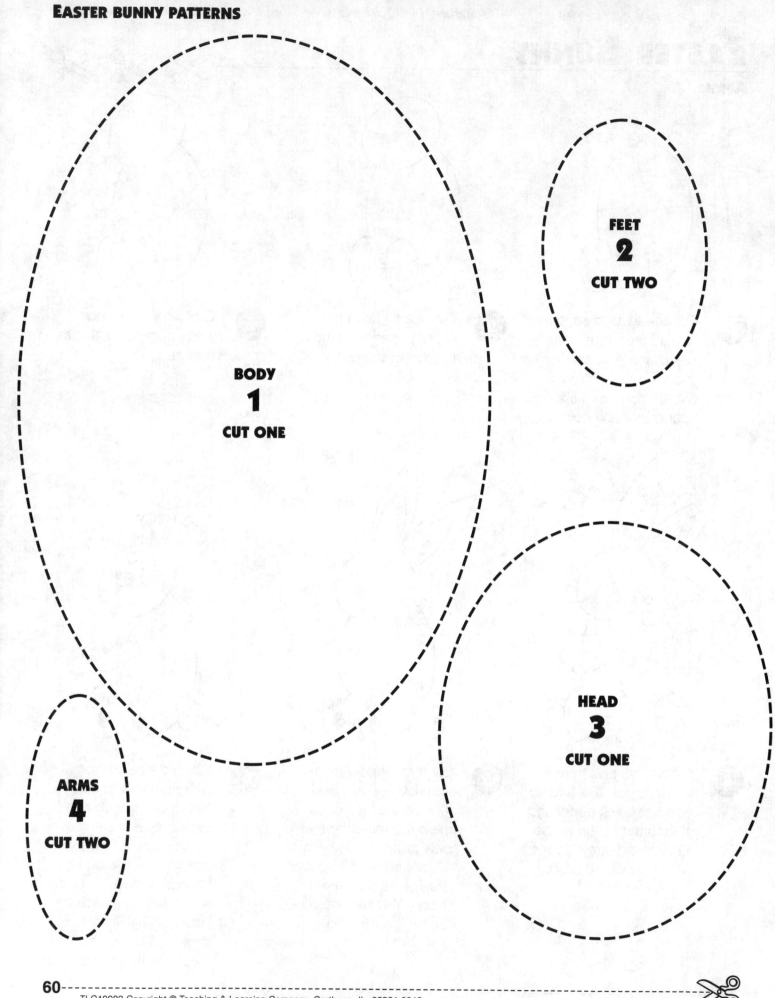

FEET
2
CUT TWO

BODY
1
CUT ONE

HEAD
3
CUT ONE

ARMS
4
CUT TWO

EASTER BUNNY PATTERNS

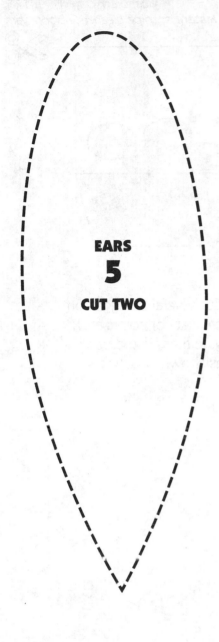

EARS
5
CUT TWO

EARS
6
CUT TWO

PAW PRINTS
7
CUT TWO

TAIL
8
CUT SEVERAL

EYES
9
CUT TWO

PUPILS
10
CUT TWO

NOSE
11
CUT ONE

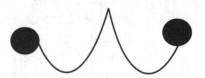

Note:
This is how the bunny's mouth is
rendered. Use this to trace or copy.

Materials: *brown or tan, lavender, light green, light yellow, orange, pale blue or white, pink and sky blue paper; scissors; glue; black crayon or marker*

Optional Materials: *pipe cleaners, ribbon, yarn*

EASTER BASKET

APRIL

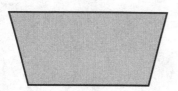

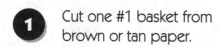

1 Cut one #1 basket from brown or tan paper.

2 Cut several #2 eggs from a variety of colors and glue them in the basket as shown.

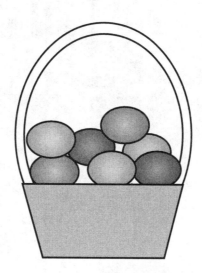

3 Add a pipe cleaner or yarn handle to the basket. A bow made from ribbon or yarn could also be glued or tied onto the basket. This is what your finished Easter basket should look like.

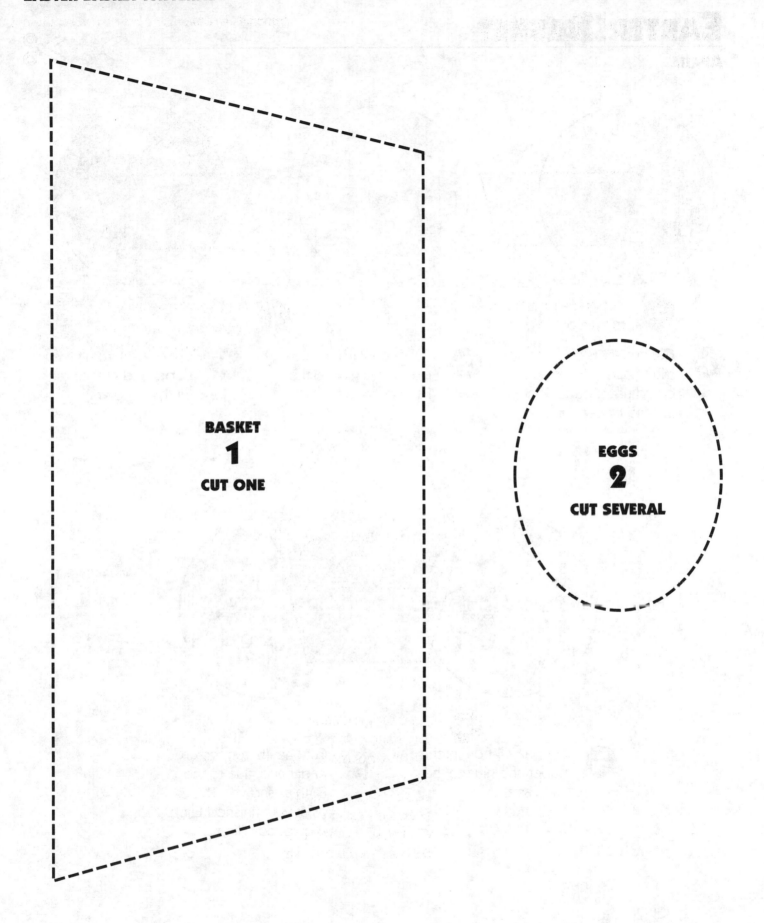

BASKET
1
CUT ONE

EGGS
2
CUT SEVERAL

Materials: blue and green paper, scissors, glue

EARTH DAY

APRIL

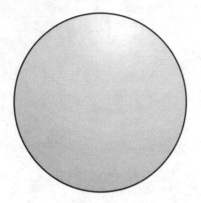 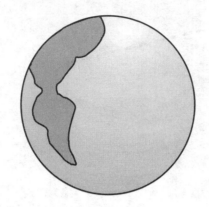 

1 Cut one #1 Earth from blue paper. (Note: You could use a paper plate instead of using #1.)

2 Cut one #2 from green paper and glue to the Earth as shown.

3 Cut one #3 from green paper and glue to the Earth as shown.

4 Cut one #4 from green paper and glue to the Earth as shown.

5 Cut one #5 from green paper and glue to the Earth as shown. This is what your finished Earth should look like.

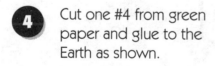

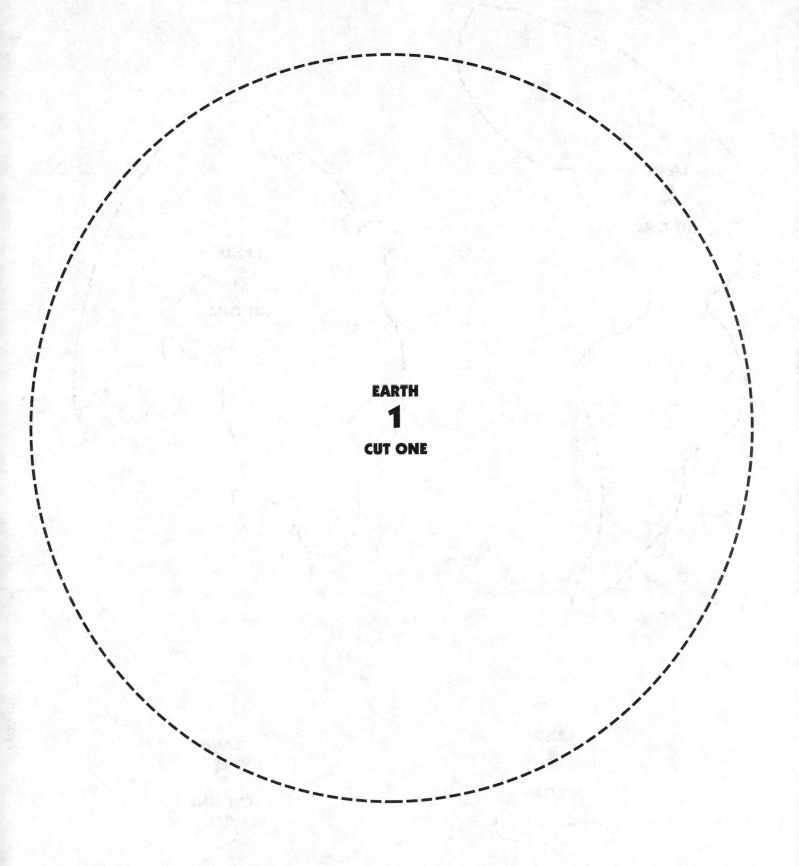

EARTH

1

CUT ONE

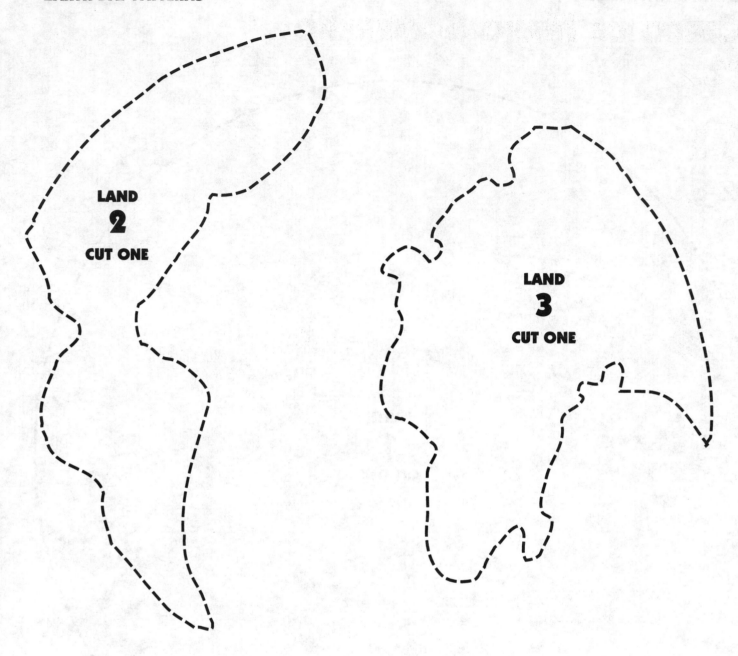

LAND
2
CUT ONE

LAND
3
CUT ONE

LAND
4
CUT ONE

LAND
5
CUT ONE

Materials: *green, purple, red and yellow paper; scissors; glue; black crayon or marker*

CINCO DE MAYO SOMBRERO

MAY

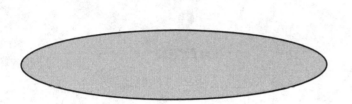

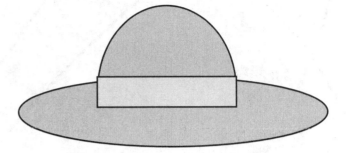

1 Cut one #1 brim from red paper.

2 Cut one #2 hat from red paper. Cut one #3 band from yellow paper and glue to the bottom of the hat. Then glue to the brim.

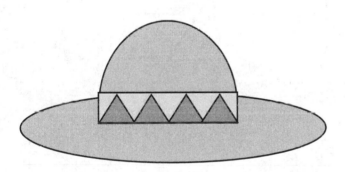

3 Cut four #4 triangles from green paper and glue on the hat band as shown.

4 Cut nine #5 circles from purple paper and glue to the back side of the bottom of the brim.

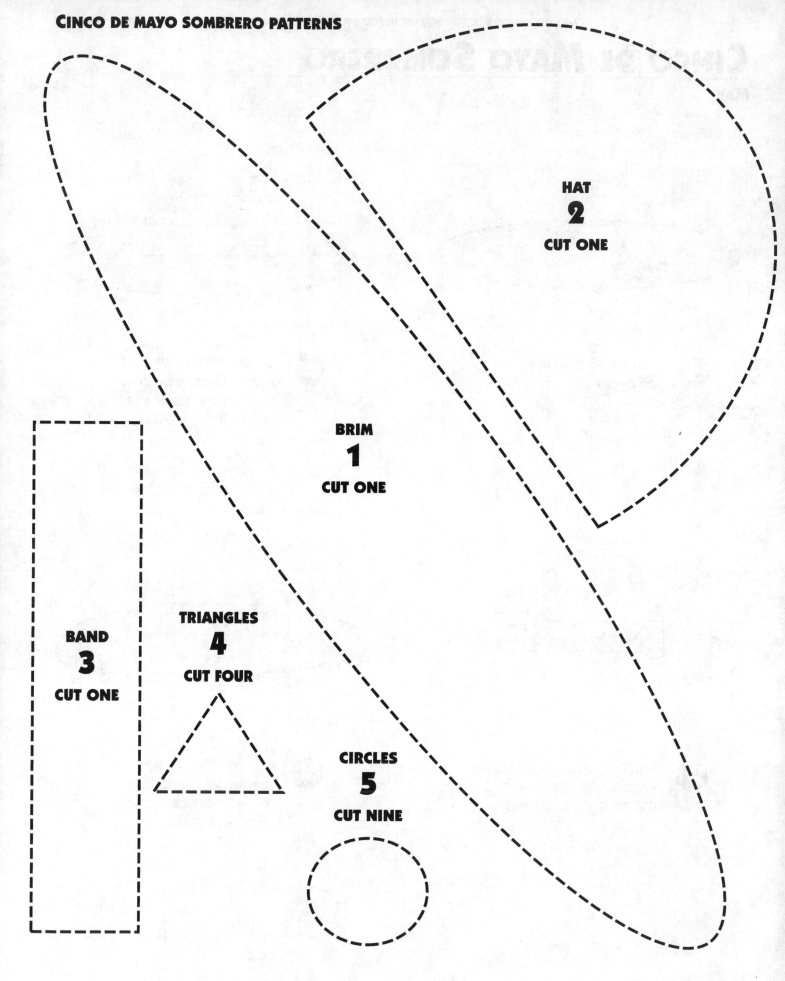

HAT
2
CUT ONE

BRIM
1
CUT ONE

BAND
3
CUT ONE

TRIANGLES
4
CUT FOUR

CIRCLES
5
CUT NINE

Cinco de Mayo Serape

MAY

Note: Instructions are given for the design pictured below. You may wish to provide children with stripes, triangles, diamonds and circles in a variety of colors and let them create their own designs.

1 Cut one #1 serape from red paper.

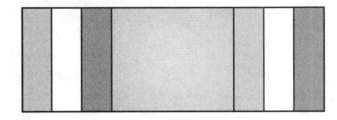

2 Cut four #2 bands from white (two) and green (two). Glue the bands at either end in the pattern: red, white, green.

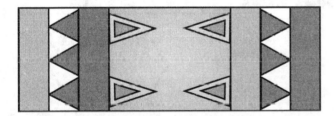

3 Cut six #3 triangles from turquoise and glue to the white band. Cut four #4 triangles from yellow and glue to the serape as shown. Cut four #5 triangles from purple and glue in the middle of the #4 triangles.

4 Cut one #6 diamond from green paper and glue in the middle of the serape. Cut four #7 circles from yellow paper and glue two to each of the green bands. Cut fourteen #8 tassels from purple and glue seven to each end. (Note: You could substitute yarn for the tassels.)

CINCO DE MAYO SERAPE PATTERNS

BANDS
2
CUT FOUR

SERAPE
1
CUT ONE

TRIANGLES FOR WHITE BAND
3
CUT SIX

TRIANGLES FOR GREEN BAND
4
CUT FOUR

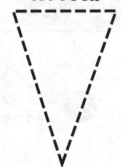

TRIANGLES FOR #4 PIECES
5
CUT FOUR

DIAMOND
6
CUT ONE

CIRCLES
7
CUT THREE

TASSELS
8
CUT FOURTEEN

Materials: *green, orange, red, white and yellow paper; scissors; glue; black crayon or marker*

MAY DAY FLOWERPOT
MAY

1 Cut one #1 base from orange or clay-colored paper.

2 Cut one #2 rim from orange or clay-colored paper. Glue to the top of the base.

3 Cut four #3 leaves from green paper and glue in place as shown.

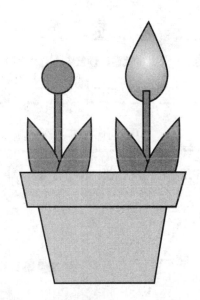

4 Cut two #4 stems from green paper and glue the stems in the center of each set of leaves.

5 Cut three #5 tulip petals from red paper. Glue one petal to one stem. Cut one #6 daisy center from yellow or orange paper and glue to the other stem.

6 Glue the other two #5 tulip petals to each side of the middle one as shown. Cut eight #7 daisy petals from white paper and glue to the back side around the #6 center.

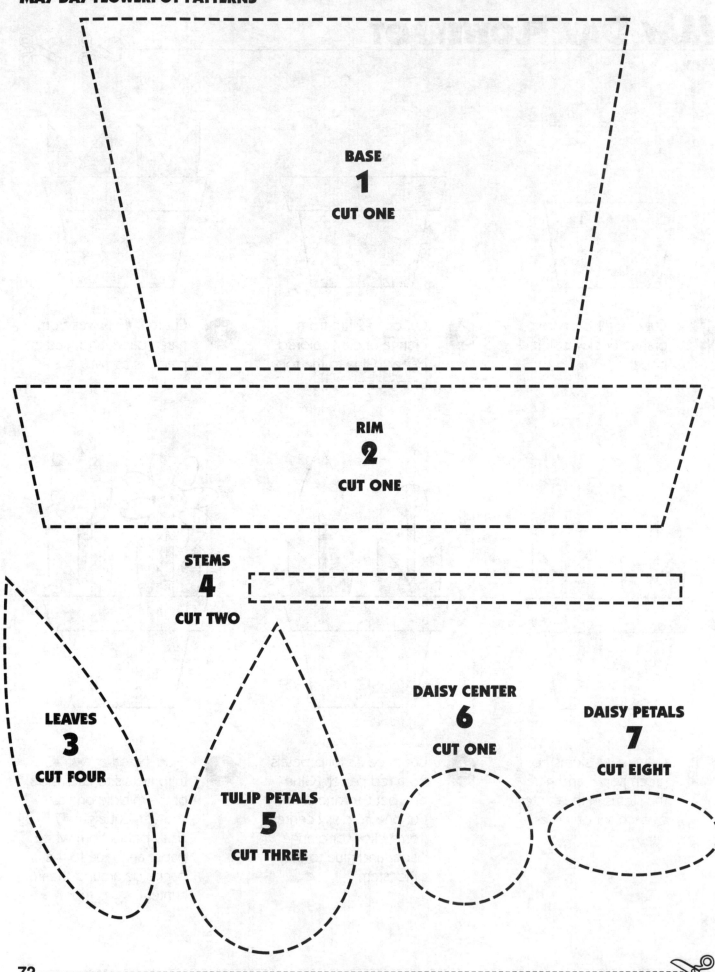

MAY DAY FLOWERPOT PATTERNS

BASE
1
CUT ONE

RIM
2
CUT ONE

STEMS
4
CUT TWO

LEAVES
3
CUT FOUR

TULIP PETALS
5
CUT THREE

DAISY CENTER
6
CUT ONE

DAISY PETALS
7
CUT EIGHT

Materials: black, green and pink or melon paper; scissors; glue; black crayon or marker

MOTHER'S DAY

MAY

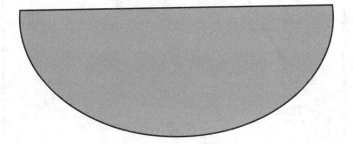

1 Cut one #1 melon rind from green paper.

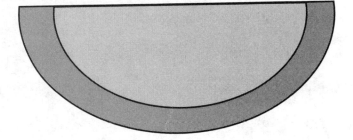

2 Cut one #2 melon from pink or melon-colored paper.

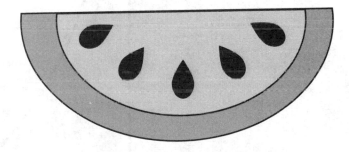

3 Glue the seeds on as shown. (Note: You may want to glue on real melon seeds.)

Directions for a Pin: Reduce melon pieces 25 to 35% depending on the size you want. Follow the directions to assemble. Use a clear glue sealant to make it shine. Glue a pin to the back when dry.

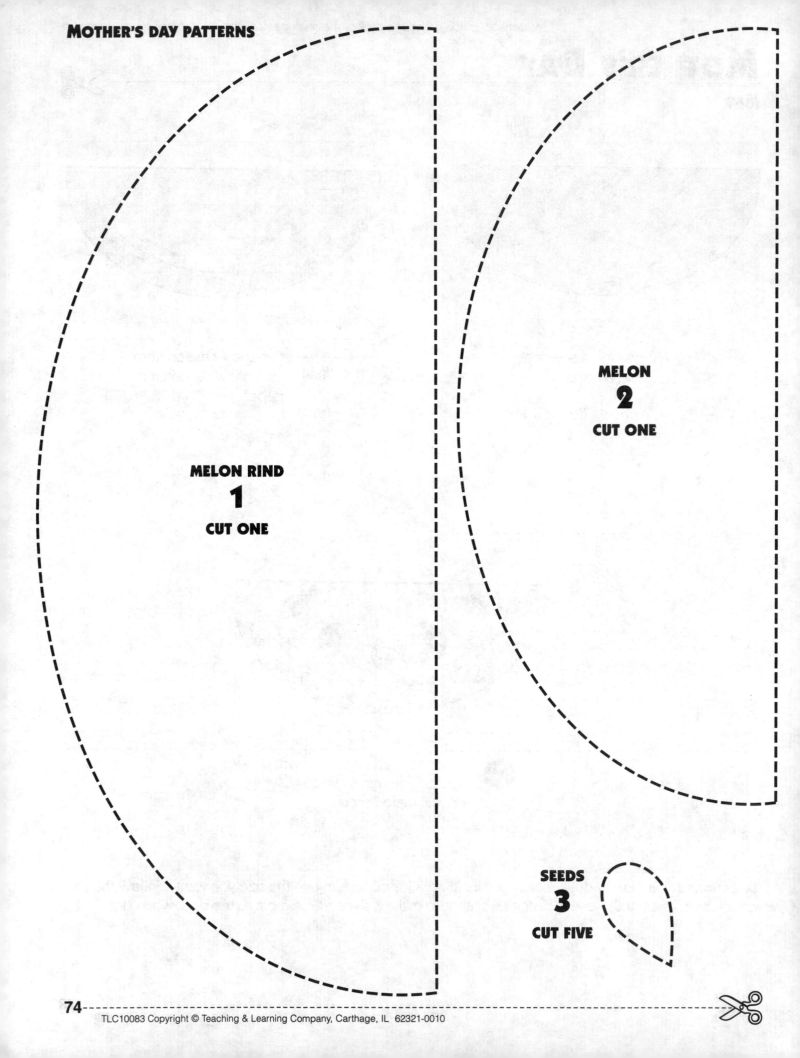

MELON
2
CUT ONE

MELON RIND
1
CUT ONE

SEEDS
3
CUT FIVE

FLAG DAY

JUNE

1 Cut one #1 flag from red paper.

2 Cut six #2 stripes from white paper. Glue the white stripes onto the red flag. Be sure to space stripes evenly.

3 Cut one #3 field from blue paper. Glue to the upper left-hand corner of the flag.

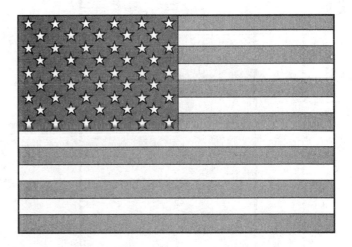

4 Place 50 stars in alternating rows of six and five on the blue field.

FLAG
1
CUT ONE

STRIPES **2** CUT FIVE

FIELD
3
CUT ONE

Materials: black, brown, two or three shades of green and white paper; scissors; glue; string; black crayon or marker
Optional Materials: glitter glue

FATHER'S DAY

JUNE

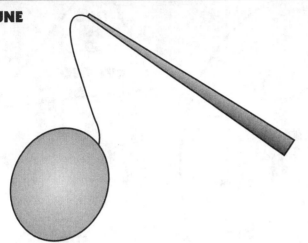

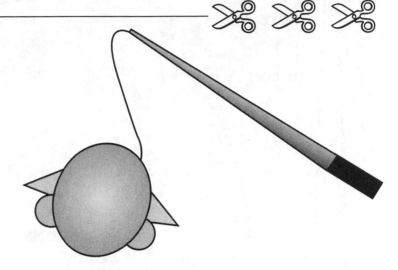

1 Cut one #1 pole from brown paper. Cut one #2 fish from green paper. Use string or yarn for fishing line. Attach to the pole. Attach the fish.

2 Cut two #3 fins and two #4 fins from a lighter shade of green. Glue one set to the back of the fish on either side of body as shown. Cut one #5 handle from black paper and glue to the end of the pole.

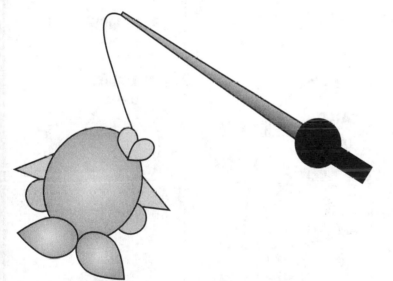

3 Cut two #6 tails from the same color paper as the fish. Glue these to the bottom of the fish as shown. Cut two #7 fish lips from lighter green and glue in place. Cut one #8 reel from black paper and glue over the handle and pole.

4 Cut one #9 center of reel from white paper and glue in the middle of the reel. Cut one #10 fin from lighter green than the fish and glue to the middle of the fish. Cut one #11 eye from black paper and glue as shown.

Note: Glitter glue can add sparkle to the fins and tail!

FATHER'S DAY PATTERNS

POLE
1
CUT ONE

FISH
2
CUT ONE

FINS
3
CUT TWO

FINS
4
CUT TWO

FISH LIPS
7
CUT TWO

HANDLE
5
CUT ONE

TAILS
6
CUT TWO

CENTER OF REEL
9
CUT ONE

FIN
10
CUT ONE

EYE
11
CUT ONE

REEL
8
CUT ONE

Materials: *blue, red, white and yellow paper; scissors; glue; black crayon or marker*

FOURTH OF JULY

1 Cut one #1 firecracker from red paper.

2 Cut one #2 wick from white paper. Glue to the top of the firecracker.

3 Cut two #3 sparks from yellow paper. Cut one #4 spark from white paper. Glue the sparks as shown.

4 Cut three #5 bands from blue paper and glue as shown.

Note: Use one half of a paper towel tube for the firecracker. Paint or cover with paper. Use foil wrapping paper for the sparks or cover with glue and glitter.

FOURTH OF JULY PATTERNS

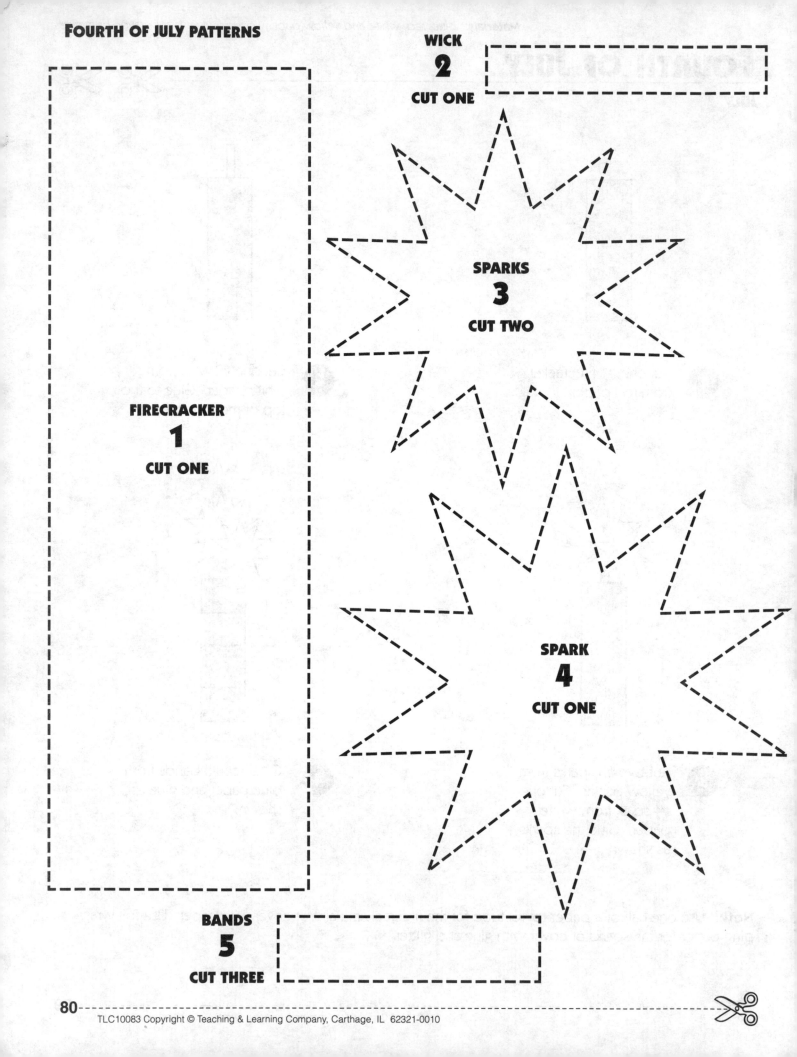

WICK
2
CUT ONE

SPARKS
3
CUT TWO

FIRECRACKER
1
CUT ONE

SPARK
4
CUT ONE

BANDS
5
CUT THREE